Rumble Road

Untold Stories from Outside the Ring

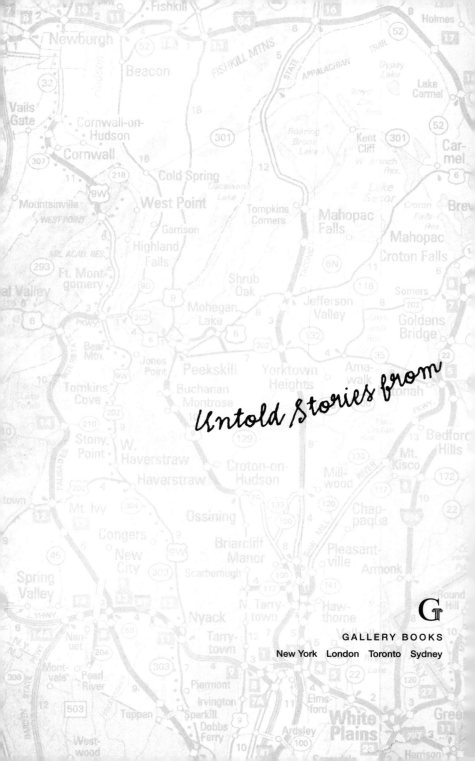

Untold Stories from

G

GALLERY BOOKS

New York   London   Toronto   Sydney

Rumble
Road

Outside the Ring

Jon Robinson

World
Wrestling
Entertainment®
BOOKS

Gallery Books
A Division of Simon & Schuster, Inc.
1230 Avenue of the Americas
New York, NY 10020

This book is a publication of Gallery Books, a division of Simon & Schuster, Inc., under exclusive license from World Wrestling Entertainment, Inc.

First Gallery Books trade paperback edition July 2010

GALLERY BOOKS and colophon are trademarks of Simon & Schuster, Inc.

For information about special discounts for bulk purchases, please contact Simon & Schuster Special Sales at 1-866-506-1949 or business@simonandschuster.com.

The Simon & Schuster Speakers Bureau can bring authors to your live event. For more information or to book an event, contact the Simon & Schuster Speakers Bureau at 1-866-248-3049 or visit our website at www.simonspeakers.com.

Manufactured in the United States of America

10   9   8   7   6   5   4   3   2   1

Library of Congress Cataloging-in-Publication Data

Robinson, Jon.
    Rumble road : untold stories from outside the ring / Jon Robinson.
      p. cm.
    1. Wrestling—Anecdotes. 2. Wrestlers. I. Title.
    GV1195.R73   2010
    796.812—dc22   2010000398

ISBN 978-1-4391-8257-4
ISBN 978-1-4391-8258-1 (ebook)

HUMBOLDT PARK

Contents

Fishkill
Holmes
Newburgh
Beacon
FISHKILL MTNS.
APPALACHIAN TRAIL
STATE
Gypsy Lake
Lake Carmel
Vails Gate
Cornwall-on-Hudson
Cornwall
Roaring Brook Lake
Kent Cliff
W. Branch Res.
Cold Spring
Oscawana Lake
Lake Secor
Mountainville
WEST POINT
West Point
Tompkins Corners
Mahopac Falls
Croton Falls Res.
Garrison
Mahopac
Highland Falls
MIL. ACAD. RES.
Croton Falls
Ft. Montgomery
TACONIC
Shrub Oak
Somers
Mohegan Lake
Jefferson Valley
Goldens Bridge
Bear Mtn.
Jones Point
Peekskill
Yorktown Heights
Amawalk
Katonah
Tomkins Cove
Buchanan
Montrose
PKWY.
Stony Point
W. Haverstraw
Haverstraw
Croton-on-Hudson
Mill-wood
Mt. Kisco
Bedford Hills
PALISADES
Mt. Ivy
Ossining
Chappaqua
Congers
Briarcliff Manor
Pleasantville
New City
SAW MILL
Armonk
Spring Valley
Scarborough
N. Tarrytown
Hawthorne
Nyack
Valhalla
Tarrytown
Nanuet
Pearl River
Montvale
Piermont
Irvington
Elmsford
Tappan
Sparkill
Dobbs Ferry
White Plains
Ardsley
Westwood
Harrison
GARDEN STATE PKWY.
N.Y.
N.J.
CONN.

It's my first road trip with WWE and I'm lost. And when I say lost, I mean lost in the GPS-actually-shows-two-arrows-pointing-directly-at-each-other-like-I'm-somehow-about-to-crash-into-myself lost. But it's not just the signs that read "Wrong Way" and "Do Not Enter" that are freaking me out. It's the fact that while everyone in the car is frantically trying to search for alternate directions on an iPhone that can't catch a signal, a light inside the car pops on to warn us of low tire pressure. And of course, when we stop at the gas station to check our tires, fill up, and catch our breaths (not to mention catch that satellite signal), the gas cap of the car actually shatters into three pieces as we simply twist the top to the left. So now not only is our GPS still freaking out, we're about to run out of gas and might have a flat.

This all happened over the course of what should have been a simple three-hour drive and back between Pittsburgh and Penn State. A trip that should've been a quick trek along scenic roads but turned into start-and-stop traffic along countless construction sites, and the only things even mildly scenic were the crazy sideshow-like attractions in the random parking lots of strip clubs and adult video complexes we passed along the way.

"Welcome to our world!" MVP laughs when I tell him about the trip. "I actually had a meeting with Vince McMahon once where we were talking about my career, and I explained to him that wrestling is my passion, it's my craft and I love it. I'm one of the guys who worked the indies and would drive five hundred miles for five dollars just for the chance to perfect my craft and work in front of a crowd. What I explained to Mr. McMahon is this: What I do in front of our audience, I do it for free. What I charge Vince McMahon for is all my time on the road. It's the grueling air travel, the car rides, and the bus rides. I charge for travel. I don't charge for performing. The travel is the real work of this business."

And judging by my one experience between shows,

he's absolutely right: Once you get to the arena, once you step inside that environment, that's when the adrenaline kicks in, that's when the excitement of the spectacle takes you away from all your broken gas caps and wonky GPS machines. Once you get to the show, that's when the fun really starts.

"People think it's all glitz and glamour, that we're jet-setting around the world," adds Christian, "but the reality is, we fly into a city, rent a car, find a restaurant, find a gym, go to the hotel, find the arena, perform at the show, find somewhere to eat after the show, and either drive on to the next town or spend the night in that hotel and drive off to the airport the next morning. Rinse and repeat. It's the same thing over and over. Sometimes we get lucky when we're overseas and we might get to spend an extra day in one place and go sightseeing, but for the most part, we're in and we're out. It's all about getting to the next arena and entertaining. That's what we live for. That's what we do. Everything else in between is just a means to an end of getting to that arena in order to perform for our fans."

And the more I was able to talk to these stars about their lives of 200-plus travel days a year, the more I kept hearing the same word pop up over and over again: *family*. These Superstars spend so much time traveling across the world in order to entertain their fans that their second families are their fellow men and women in tights, performing together in a raucous show CM Punk describes as a "rock concert where the band is beating each other up on stage while at the same time performing improv comedy."

But maybe nobody better sums up what it means to live your life out of a suitcase traveling alongside everyone from a leprechaun to a Glamazon to a king better than second-generation wrestler Cody Rhodes.

"Life on the road is a unique thing. It's such an experience because you're taking a bunch of different people from different parts of the world with different life experiences, who come from different social circles and have very different behaviors," he says. "But you get all of these people on the road together and they become a family very quickly. It's a lot like a real family. It's not necessarily people you like very much or you want to hang out with on your off days, but we all certainly depend on each other.

"There is a long-standing tradition in wrestling, that when you get to the building, you shake hands with everybody. People have forgotten why we do that, but I am very fortunate to know because I was reminded regularly by my old man [WWE Hall of Famer Dusty Rhodes]. It is just a way of saying thank you. What you have to realize is that the top is not just one person. It takes two. You need someone in the ring. You need someone to work against. You need someone to work with.

"So when we travel on the road, I see it as family because that's truly who we are."

Rumble Road follows some of this WWE family as they dish the dirt on some of their most memorable stories between performances. From their favorite practical jokes to the shenanigans that happen at three in the morning to the time Santino punched a Tasmanian Devil and made her cry, here are some of the funniest moments straight from the Superstars who lived them.

Now if only I can get this GPS working again, maybe I can get back on the road for another trip of my own. And I still don't understand how a gas cap shatters into three pieces. . . .

Rumble Road

Untold Stories from Outside the Ring

Fishkill
Newburgh
Beacon
Holmes
Lake Carmel
Carmel
FISHKILL MTNS.
APPALACHIAN TRAIL
STATE
Gypsy Lake
Boyd Cor. Res.
Vails Gate
Cornwall-on-Hudson
Cornwall
Roaring Brook Lake
Kent Cliff
W. Branch Res.
Cold Spring
Oscawana Lake
Lake Secor
Mountainville
WEST POINT
West Point
Garrison
Tompkins Corners
Mahopac Falls
Croton Falls Res.
Mahopac
Croton Falls
MIL. ACAD. RES.
Highland Falls
TACONIC
Ft. Montgomery
Shrub Oak
Jefferson Valley
Somers
Mohegan Lake
Goldens Bridge
PKWY.
Bear Mtn.
Jones Point
Peekskill
Yorktown Heights
Amawalk
Katonah
INTERSTATE
Tomkins Cove
Buchanan
Montrose
Stony Point
W. Haverstraw
Haverstraw
Croton-on-Hudson
Millwood
Bedford Hills
Mt. Kisco
PALISADES
RIVER
Mt. Ivy
Ossining
Chappaqua
Congers
SAW MILL
Briarcliff Manor
Pleasantville
New City
Armonk
Spring Valley
Scarborough
Round Hill
THWY.
Nyack
N. Tarrytown
Hawthorne
Valhalla
Nanuet
Tarrytown
CONN.
N.Y.
N.J.
PKWY.
Montvale
Pearl River
Piermont
Elmsford
Irvington
GARDEN STATE
Tappan
Sparkill
White Plains
Dobbs Ferry
Ardsley
Westwood
Scarsdale
Harrison

One

Ribs

"Don't ever fall asleep first. If I had one piece of advice for

future wrestlers traveling in groups, that would be it."

—CHRISTIAN

Forget everything you know about curved bones and barbecue

sauce. When it comes to the world of sports entertainment,

any type of practical joke or prank is referred to as a rib. It can

be wrestler on wrestler, wrestler on wrestler's car, wrestler

on entire backstage, and even wrestler on poor convenience

store clerk who just happens to be working at three in the

morning. ✪ Whatever the combination, the amount of effort

and thought that goes into some of these setups (some

unfold over months!) is downright amazing, but there's no

denying, the results are hilarious. ✪ "We like to have fun

with each other, and the ribs are all in good fun," explains Kofi

Kingston with his trademark smile. "But once you rib somebody, you have to expect to get ribbed back, and it's probably going to be worse than the rib you did, so it kind of keeps spiraling. It tends to get out of control at times, but I try to stay out of the whole ribbing scene just because I don't want to be ribbed. But we're on the road so much, we have to find something to keep ourselves entertained, otherwise it'll just be us driving on the road listening to boring conversations and bad radio."

So here they are, the best road ribs in recent WWE history. Ever hear the one about Chris Jericho's deaf music fan?

Can You Hear Me Now?

Christian

Back when I was in the Independents, I had this manager in Detroit who was deaf. And basically, if someone who is deaf wants to call you on the phone, they call this other person first and they type in what they want to say. This other person then reads what is typed word for word almost like a translator. They have to say the words exactly like it is written to them, no matter what it says. So back in the day, this manager used to rib me all the time and he'd call me throughout the week with his deaf telephone interpreter and he would say these really rude things. He'd use language not befitting a woman, and this poor woman operator would have to say it to me word for word. I'd have to respond, and I would be so embarrassed listening to this woman that I'd just give one-word answers. Yes. No. Maybe. That's all I'd ever say because all I wanted to do was get off the phone as soon as possible. It was so embarrassing, and this manager just got a big kick out of it because he knew how uncomfortable it made me.

Anyway, out of the blue years later, I get a call and it's the same sort of thing happening. I figured out right away that someone was trying to pull a rib on me, so I hung up and I immediately looked up the area code where this number came from. The number was a Minnesota area code, so I scrolled through my phone and looked to see who I knew from Minnesota. There was only one wrestler . . . Daivari. So I called him up and said, "Why are you trying to rib me, kid? You're just a rookie here." All of a sudden he got so quiet, so I told him, "Hey, you didn't answer my question."

He started apologizing, but I told him it was all right. All I wanted to know is if he told anyone what he was up to. When he told me no, I asked him to help me rib Chris Jericho.

So for months and months and months, Chris was

with his group Fozzy, and we pretended we were a deaf fan of him and his music from England named Gertrude and we'd contact him using this same deaf translating service. We said that we got his number, and even though we attended all his concerts and we couldn't hear him actually sing, we just knew he had a beautiful voice and we could tell that he was singing to me. We even went so far as to have Gertrude say that she told her mom about him and her mom told her it might be a long shot, but that she should go after him and try to make the relationship work. What's funny is, Chris would come up to me and tell me what she'd said during the call and he'd ask me if I knew anything about this. He'd tell me how he had this crazy fan who loves his music and loves his words but she's deaf. He was really starting to get freaked out. And then any time we'd head to England, we'd really crank up the calls. We'd hide around the corner and watch him answer his phone. He'd talk for a second, hang up his phone, and then we'd see him sitting there just shaking his head. So we'd call back and we'd see him look at the caller ID and he wouldn't want to answer it, he'd just put the phone away and pretend it wasn't ringing.

We actually had this going on for months until we finally let the cat out of the bag and told him it was us. He got a pretty good laugh out of it. The funniest moment was probably when we called and told him that Gertrude was going to his concert and that after the show she was going to head to the hotel so they could finally meet and talk about things, talk about their future together. You'd see him walking through the lobby of our hotel and he'd be looking side to side as he hurried to the elevator. The look on his face was too funny. I think he was really scared this deaf stalker was going to jump out at him from the elevator or something.

Yeah I Hear You, But That's Not the Whole Story

Chris Jericho

When Christian was off one time for an injury, for some reason I got this e-mail about celebrity phone calls. It was this service where you could get various celebrities to call you on your birthday or for a special occasion or whatever it was. And one of the names on the list was this guy named Lash LeRoux. He was listed as a "WCW Wrestling Superstar" . . . he was in WCW for like five minutes and he had this really bad Cajun gimmick that always made Christian and me laugh. He'd talk like he was "Cay-jon," the

"Cay-jon" man. So I signed up for the celebrity birthday call, and you could choose the celebrity you wanted, and these celebrities were like Frank Stallone, Todd Bridges, Urkel, and Lash LeRoux. So I signed up for Lash LeRoux, and in the e-mail, you could type in the message you wanted to send. So I wrote: "To little Jason Reso [Christian's real name], I hear you're not feeling good. Keep your head up, buddy. We're all pulling for you, little trouper." So Jay was at home and he got the call: "Hey, this is Lash LeRoux!" Jay was like, "Yeah?" And Lash went through the message, like, "Hey little buddy, hope your knee feels better soon," then he hangs up after like fifteen seconds. That was Christian's celebrity call, and that was the reason he wanted to get his revenge with the deaf fan/stalker. It's because I got him first with the Lash LeRoux celebrity birthday call. That's what started it off.

But the thing about the deaf calls, he had the woman sounding like a complete psycho. He was having her say *Fatal Attraction*–type stuff, about how we were meant to be together, and I kept getting these calls every couple of weeks that would just get progressively crazier and crazier and crazier. And the one I remember most is this time when I was on a bus in England. Christian was on a different bus, but they had pulled up next to each other, so he was watching my reaction when his deaf stalker was saying things like, "Just because I'm three hundred and fifty pounds doesn't mean I'm not beautiful." And what's funny is, I didn't even know you could do this. The operator literally has to say whatever the message is, so the operator is saying everything so stoically, but what he's saying is things like, "I'm going to come to your room and bury this knife in your chest if you don't want to have sex with me." It was crazy. And this one time when we were sitting on the bus, he could see me through the window being like, "What the hell is going on?" It was insane.

The Get Back

Shelton Benjamin

Everyone knows that character-wise, I've had my problems with Cryme Tyme, but some of the problems extend outside the show as well. Like one night after a Pay-Per-View in Indianapolis, traffic was crazy and we were all trying to get out of the building. I'm trying to navigate through the crowd and through traffic, and as I pull up to the light, Cryme Tyme was in the car next to me. We're pretty good at ribbing each other, so just for the heck of it, I threw an empty bottle of water from my car right into their car through an open window. We were all laughing and everything, and I pull away. But when I stop at the next light, I see Cryme Tyme pull up behind me and Shad gets out of the car. He runs up to my car and pours a complete bottle of some sort of chocolate protein shake over my windshield. It was so thick, even when I turn my wipers on, I can't get this stuff off and I can't even see through my windshield. I actually needed to pull over to a gas station a few blocks down the street just to clean this shake off, and there was chocolate everywhere. It was at that point I gave them a warning that there would be payback.

So about two or three weeks later, there was a super show in Nassau, and myself and one other wrestler stopped before the show and bought a couple of quarts of oil, peanut butter, and a down pillow. While Cryme Tyme were in the ring, me and this other gentleman proceeded to go out and pour the oil all over their car. Then we ripped the feathers out of the pillow and put the feathers all over the top of the car, all over the backseat, all over the front seat, and I spread peanut butter all over the steering wheel and the handles. It was a complete mess.

When Cryme Tyme came out and saw the car, they couldn't believe what happened. But as it turned out, it wasn't their car. They were actually riding with Primo, so poor Primo just got caught in the cross fire. The funny thing is, Cryme Tyme started yelling, "Ha-ha, you tried to get us, but you didn't get us!" And I was like, "Okay, so what you're saying then is you're still in my crosshairs." And they both look at each other, then they turn to me at the same time and were like, "Yeah, you're right. You got us."

I ended up paying Primo for the car to be cleaned, but it was worth it.

Boom Boom Pow

Randy Orton

We were in Tijuana about three years ago, and Revolution Avenue is notorious down there for all their little shops and clubs and strip bars and the craziness going on. I used to frequent that area when I was in the Marine Corps, back in 1999. All of us guys would go down there, taking the bus to San Diego, then taking the trolley to the border at San Ysidro and finally taking a cab to Revolution Avenue. It took about three hours for us to get there from base, but it was worth it. It was a ton of fun. Now I come back there all these years later, only now I'm a WWE wrestler. Back in the Marine Corps, no one bothered us. Now there are like a hundred kids following us up and down the street. It's crazy.

That night, we found a shop that sold fireworks. Not your normal little Fourth of July fireworks. These were quarter sticks of dynamite. And I'm not just calling these things quarter sticks of dynamite, these were legit *quarter sticks of dynamite* . . . these things would blow your hands off. They were eight inches long with a twenty- or thirty-second wick on them that burned slow just so you could run away. They were nuts and they were only like eight bucks each, so I bought a dozen of them.

Later that night, we were doing a show outdoors at this bullfighting arena that was probably a century old if not more, and the place was huge. They had all of these little pits where they kept the bulls, but the pits were empty and they had all of this loose dirt, so a couple of us dug this big hole and put a quarter stick of dynamite underneath. And this fuse was so long that we were able to use some old shovels lying around and bury this thing pretty deep. Before this, we had lit a few off just to see what they could do, and man, were they dangerous! But this one that we buried, dirt went flying everywhere and the noise was just unbelievable. It sounded like a bomb went off. The vibrations and the percussions of this arena with 20,000 seats and all of the old stone and cement of this bullfighting arena . . . the walls shook when this thing exploded.

The thing is, we had a lot of *policia* down at the arena.

The Mexican police were guarding the building outside and keeping order with all of the big mobs of people who were lining up to come in. All of these *policia* were armed with machine guns and pistols, and they heard this big boom and they all drew their weapons and ran inside. It was total chaos.

I thought I was going to get in trouble when they found out what I was doing, especially when you see all of these guys with machine guns running in your direction, but it ended up that they all thought it was funny . . . so we did it again.

At that point, Santino and I put our heads together and came up with the idea that we should act like I got arrested. So they handcuffed me and dragged me out like they were arresting me for lighting the dynamite. We actually walked through the backstage area with me in handcuffs, and I just kept my head down, like, "Damn, what have I gotten myself into." Nobody knew what to think. They all thought I got arrested by the Mexican police, which is definitely not something you ever want to do.

Miz Gets Down to Basics

Ted DiBiase

You need to be strong-willed and mentally tough for this life on the road or it will catch up with you. You need to eat right and train and you're away from your family, so if you don't love sports entertainment, if you're not passionate about it, there's no way you can do it. But the fans are amazing, and they make all of the travel and everything that goes along with it totally worth it. It's tougher than people think because we're not just traveling on Mondays and one Sunday a month. We're traveling from town to town, and we're not driven, we drive ourselves. We have to find hotel rooms, we live out of a suitcase, and you see the world out of a window. It's hard, but it's worth it. It's especially worth it when we're all together in the same hotel and something happens that just makes you laugh harder than you could ever expect.

I remember this one night we were all in France. We were all sitting down eating inside the hotel at the restaurant after the show, and it was late. It was the last night of our tour, and we were all just hanging out and talking. When it's our last night of a long tour like this, we don't usually sleep that night because then you can just sleep easier on the plane the next day. So most of us were down in the restaurant along with Hornswoggle. He's a funny guy as it is, but he was ready to cause some trouble that night. He's asking everyone, "Where is The Miz?" We were all looking for The Miz, but The Miz had already gone to bed. So Hornswoggle leans over to me and he's like, "Teddy, we need to go find The Miz and wake him up. We need to do something to him." We didn't know what we wanted to do, but one thing we knew, we already had stolen the key to his room from earlier in the night. So we go up to his room, and Hornswoggle was carrying this giant bottle of water. I was actually just there to protect the little guy in case The Miz tried to kill him. I was his bodyguard.

So we go up there, and all the lights were out. Hornswoggle sneaks into his room, and while The Miz was sound asleep, he dumps the entire bottle of water over The Miz's bed. Miz jumps out of bed, Hornswoggle starts to run out of the room, I'm running behind him, and Miz is running after us, and he chucks this bottle of water at us as we race down the hall. But what's funny is, The Miz is running down the hall and all he's wearing is his underwear, and I swear, we all stop at the same time and hear the door behind him go *click*. So now Miz has been woken up, he's just had water poured all over him, and he's locked out of his hotel room half naked. Hornswoggle and I then head down to the hotel lobby and tell all the boys to gather around and watch what's about to happen, as the only way Miz could get back in his room was to go up to the woman at the front desk . . . we weren't going to do it for him.

So The Miz walks down, and while he's trying to figure out what to do soaking wet and half naked, we realize that we still have the key to his room. I tell Hornswoggle that I'll stall The Miz while he goes back up to his room and finishes the job. Miz was a pretty good sport about it, walking off the elevator in front of all of the boys while everyone was laughing at him, and he actually sat down in the lobby for a minute in his underwear. But while he was doing that, Hornswoggle used his key to get back in the room and he stole all of The Miz's clothes, all of his towels, all of his sheets . . . everything! He even dumped more water on his bed and was back down before Miz got his new key. And Miz had no idea. Everyone goes back to their rooms to go pack, as we only had an hour or two at this point before we needed to leave, and Miz didn't even realize all his stuff was gone. He fell asleep for a few hours, then woke up the next morning and realized he didn't have any clothes. We made him sweat it out until we were about to leave before we told him where his clothes were. Man, the midget got him good.

permanent Ink

Christian

Don't ever fall asleep first. If I had one piece of advice for future wrestlers traveling in groups, that would be it. The reason? I was on an airplane with the Hardys and Edge. We were all on a red-eye flight from Las Vegas to Chicago, and we might have all had a little too much to drink as they say, and the flight was pretty much empty, so we were all just hanging out in the back of the plane and having some laughs. Not anything crazy, but we were just all joking around and talking. I then made the mistake of thinking I was going to sit back and relax for a couple of seconds, but instead I ended up falling asleep. I woke up when we landed, and as I stood up, I started to notice people staring at me. I was like, "Hold on here a second, something is just not right." Then I looked over at Matt and he had fallen asleep right after me, and I saw that they had taken a Sharpie and written all over his face with black ink. So I didn't say anything to Matt, I just went into the bathroom, and of course, they had written all over my face with the same Sharpie. They had drawn the people's eyebrow on me. They wrote "Dickface" across my forehead.

So I go to the bathroom of the airplane and I'm trying to scrub as hard as I could to get all of this off my face. Of course, you just can't do that great a job scrubbing the people's eyebrow off your mug in an airplane bathroom, so when I come out, now I have marker smudged all over my face. I had to walk through the airport with Sharpie smeared everywhere, and I'm sure I didn't look too great. But I did look better than Matt. Matt had no idea they had written on his face too. Not until he walked out into the airport and he realized everyone was staring at him. He finally put two and two together, that he fell asleep right after I did on the plane, and when he ran to the bathroom he found all the Sharpie drawings across his forehead too. And actually, remembering this story reminds me of something . . . I never got Edge back.

Two-for-One

Chavo Guerrero

One of the things you always need to do is keep yourself occupied, keep yourself entertained. You're always looking for something to do. That's how the ribs come into play. Just the other day, I was checking into the hotel at three in the morning and I saw a bag on the ground. One of the guys had checked in right before us but left his Adidas bag at the counter. I saw this and I figured it had to be one of the wrestlers. I asked the person at the counter, "Who just checked in?" and they told me it was Evan Bourne, Miz, Kofi, and Hornswoggle. So I convinced the lady at the desk to give me their room number. Then I called the room and pretended to be the cops. I was like, "This is Sergeant Daniels, did somebody leave an Adidas bag down here?" Miz was like, "Yeah, we did." So I told him, "Could the person whose bag it is come down and bring their ID with them? We found some illegal substances in the bag and we need to talk to you."

All of a sudden, they started freaking out and I could hear them arguing. "Did you put something in my bag?" "No!" "What are they talking about?" "Someone from the hotel must've put something in our bag!"

By the time they actually came down, they were so scared, but then they saw it was me and they started laughing. They were like, "You jerk!" They thought someone from the hotel tried to set them up or something. It was too funny.

But that wasn't the only time I got The Miz. We were riding together one time and I got pulled over for speeding. The officer looked at me and he recognized me, but he didn't recognize Miz. Then he asked me to step out of the car and walked me to the back. He was like, "You're Chavo, right?" And I told him I was, but before he could say anything else, I told him, "Help me play a rib on my friend."

He asked Miz for his license, and Miz's license was really old and you couldn't really read the expiration date or any of the info, so the cop totally played along and asked Miz to step out of the car. Then the cop really started grilling him about why his license looked like that and why he had an out-of-state ID. Miz tried to explain, but he was nervous, so I pretended to stick up for him, but the cop told me to shut up, how this didn't concern me. He really played it up good. Miz was going crazy on the side of the road, but I couldn't let it go any farther, so we told him it was a rib. It doesn't get much better than getting a North Carolina state trooper to rib The Miz. Any chance we get, we're going to get someone good, and the opportunities always seem to arise with some of these younger guys.

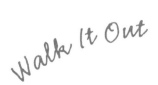

Kofi Kingston

Me and Hornswoggle travel together all the time, but I don't really let him drive because his car back home has pedal extenders that enable him to keep his feet at a normal length so that if the air bag goes off, it won't suffocate him. When we're on the road, the rental cars don't have these pedal extenders, so if he wants to drive, he literally has to pull his seat all the way up to where his chest is on the steering wheel. God forbid if we ever got into an accident and the air bag went off, he would suffocate. So I never let him drive. But whenever we travel with The Miz and Evan Bourne, they both always play it up like they want Swoggle to drive. They really try to get everyone riled up, like, "Hey, why don't you let Swoggle drive? What are you going to do about it?" But I'm like, "Look, I will not get in the car with him. Aside from his safety, I'm really concerned for our safety because Hornswoggle drives pretty recklessly. He's not what you would call a conscientious driver by any means." So I think it's safer for everyone if I do the driving . . . or if anyone but Swoggle gets behind the wheel. That's when we're the safest.

So we were all driving through Canada this one time, and Miz and Evan were busting my chops about wanting to have Swoggle drive. So when we stopped to fill up for gas, I went inside to pay, and apparently they were all conspiring the whole time to see what I would do if Swoggle got behind the wheel. So when I got out of the gas station,

Hornswoggle was in the front seat. At that same time, I saw The Miz start to get out of the car. Now, me and Hornswoggle travel and we spend so much time together that we can look at each other and start to read each other's minds. So at this point, as soon as The Miz left the car, I made eye contact with Hornswoggle and I knew exactly what to do.

Now, all this time, Miz thought he was going to rib me. He thought he was working with Hornswoggle and he was on the good side of the rib. But not for long. When Miz left the car, I jumped in and Hornswoggle took off, leaving Miz at the gas station. I thought Hornswoggle would just drive up like ten or fifteen feet and we'd all get a good laugh and let The Miz back in. But it turns out, our hotel was about a half mile away and it was directly across this highway from the gas station, so Hornswoggle just kept on driving. He left The Miz at the gas station, drove all the way to the hotel, parked the car, then we sat there and watched The Miz try to cross this busy highway on foot and make his way back to our hotel. He was out there dodging traffic, then he finally made his way to this really big field that he had to cross in order to get to the hotel. Hornswoggle made him walk back the entire way. I couldn't believe it.

It's funny because Hornswoggle can't be more than

three and a half feet tall, but he bullies The Miz. He really is a bully, and there's nothing The Miz can do about it.

Randy Orton

We were in Alabama at a tanning salon, and there were six of us: Evan Bourne, me, Santino, Chris Masters, Cody Rhodes, and Ted DiBiase. Cody was the last one in the tanning bed, and it's a common prank amongst us that if you leave that tanning bed door open while you're tanning, we'll go in there and steal your clothes. So it all started off with me finding out what room Cody was in, sneaking up, trying the door, and finding out the door was unlocked. Next thing you know, I'm in his room and I steal all of his clothes. Everyone is laughing outside, but I decide, "Let's take this a step farther." So I went back inside his room, and of course he's tanning, so he's got a towel over his face and he has no idea what is going on. So I take my foot and open the door, and there is Cody Rhodes with only a towel over his face and he's, let's just say, standing at attention. A picture was taken but we had to delete it so Cody would stop complaining. It was probably the most embarrassing moment of his life.

Rib Gone Wrong

Goldust

It was me, Owen Hart, Davey Boy Smith, and Billy Gunn, and we were driving from Montreal to Bangor, Maine. It was snowing like hell, and I was driving in this nice thick Cadillac. You can't really see the road, but it just looked so flat out on the sides, like plains. Just flat plains on both sides. So I thought this would be a good time to rib the boys and scare the crap out of them. I figured I'd pull over and just drive straight through one of these fields. The moonlight was out but you still couldn't see too far in the distance. So I got everyone talking and I'm driving pretty fast, but there was nothing around, and I mean absolutely nothing. There was this little itty-bitty general store on the right, and I pass that at about eighty miles per hour when I decide now is the time. I pull off to the right to head straight into this field. Only thing is, I was thinking it was a field, but it's really not. I ended up hitting this snowbank and all you hear is *boom-boom-boom-boom-boom!* Snow is going everywhere, and it's up over the hood—the snow was that deep. And now we're stuck. Everybody is freaking out. All I hear is, "What the hell are you doing?" and "We're going to die!"

I get out of the car, and when I see the damage, I'm like, "Damn, I just ribbed myself." I knew I wasn't going to be able to get us out of there. There wasn't anybody on the road anywhere around, but luckily for us, here comes this truck. It had to be the only truck for miles, but he saw us and pulled us out. It was lucky because this was three in the morning, and here we are stuck off on the side of a road in a snowbank. We got back in and everyone was laughing about it, but it was still really cool because I had everyone so scared. Here I was thinking it was just a field, and I almost got us all frozen to death. It could've been disastrous, but it wasn't. I guess that's what still makes it so funny.

Fixing Up Marcus

The Miz

One night we were driving, and we had about five people in our car. We were trying to find someplace to watch the Oscar De La Hoya versus Floyd "Money" Mayweather fight. We end up getting out of our car and

walking around, trying to find someplace that is showing the fight, and these guys carrying beer recognize me
from being on *The Real World*. I ask them where we can
watch the fight and they tell us to follow them through
these bushes, where we end up at this fraternity house
with about seventy people inside watching the fight. It's
standing-room-only inside the house, but these guys give
us prime seating. So we all sit down, and Marcus Cor Von
kicks back in one of the last La-Z-Boy chairs. This one guy
sees Marcus, and he sits down on one of the arms of the
chair, and he's staring at Marcus. This guy is like, "Wow,
you're big." And Marcus tells him, "Thank you very much.
Just watching the show." Then the conversation goes something like this:

"What's your name?"

"Marcus."

"What do you do?"

"I'm a professional wrestler."

"Oh really? Wow. You have such big muscles." And
this guy actually starts feeling on Marcus's biceps.

So Marcus turns to him and says, "Thank you very
much, but I'd appreciate it if you don't touch me."

"Sorry about that," the guy tells him, "but you're just
so cute."

This guy goes on like this for the entire fight, and of

course, we start egging the guy on. We tell him how Marcus is kind of shy and how you have to really warm him up. So he keeps asking Marcus if he wants something to drink, and Marcus is like, "Sure, I'd love a water." We tell the guy to get him beer because once he starts drinking a little bit, he gets really touchy-feely.

So this guy just keeps trying and trying anything he can to talk to Marcus, and Marcus is getting really upset. Literally, Marcus gets up from his chair and walks to the complete other side of the house, and the guy follows him. Finally, Marcus says that he really needs to go, but the guy really wants his phone number. So of course, we gave the guy Marcus's number, and as soon as we get to the car, Marcus starts getting these texts, like, "You're so cute!" and "You're so fun, why don't you talk to me?" Marcus had no idea who it was, but the texts kept coming and we kept laughing. Things like that can really make a long car ride seem a whole lot shorter.

Beth Phoenix

It's not the easiest thing in the world to wrestle in a bikini. We're doing some really physical things out there and trying to really lay into each other, but at the same time, we're trying to look hot. So I thought it might be fun to play a rib on Gail Kim one day by convincing her we were going to have a Bikini match.

It's always a challenge for us girls to have a match like this because you're showing so much of your body and you want to look perfect, so that involves tanner. So it's a whole big process to prepare for these matches. In fact, the less clothes you wear, the more preparation is needed.

Anyway, I found out that we were scheduled to have a tag match on *Raw*, so I decided, since there's all sorts of stress and anxiety involved in wrestling in a bikini, that I'd send a text message out to all of the girls to convince Gail that we were going to be in a Bikini match just to stress her out. So she came to TV all worried, and we let her sweat it out for a while before she finally realized that we were just having a regular match.

I've known Gail for a long time and we've had a lot of matches against each other, so it was fun to be able to get under her skin a little bit. I really wanted to let it go as long as possible, even if that meant her getting in her bikini and getting ready for the match, but unfortunately it never got that far. Maybe next time.

The Kidnapper

Shelton Benjamin

When I first got on the road with the *SmackDown!* crew, there were a lot of us traveling together. I was in a group with Charlie Haas, Rikishi, Rey Mysterio, and a few other guys . . . all together, there would be about ten of us. We would rent a few SUVs or minivans and follow each other around from town to town. But what Rey and I would do, we'd stop for gas and walk into a convenience store. Obviously, no one would know who we are because a lot of people don't recognize Rey without the mask, and at the time I was so new, I could pretty much walk around unnoticed. But me and Rey would always do this thing where, right in front of the cashier, we'd bump into each other and we'd get into it like we were about to fight. Like, "Hey man, watch where you're going!" "No, you watch where you're going!" We would get to the point where we'd be real loud and animated, and we did it just to get a rise out of the cashiers. The cashier would always be like, "Please, guys, calm down. Please don't fight in here. Just calm down." We've done it so many times, and I swear, it's the funniest thing ever when these cashiers think a fight is about to break out in their store.

The best was one time, Rey said something and I was like, "Fine, we'll see . . . I'll get you!" So I walk out of the store and hop in the van we rented. Then when Rey walked out the front door, we sped the van in front of the store, slammed on the brakes, threw the door open, and snatched Rey into the van before speeding off. We looked back and the cashier was freaking out like you couldn't believe. He thought we just kidnapped one of his customers. I don't know if he ever called the cops or what. All I know is it was funny as hell.

The Kidnappee

Rey Mysterio

What's funny about this story is, as soon as we'd bump into each other, we'd start arguing and we'd really work the whole scene good, raising our voices louder and louder the more we got into it. "Hey, watch where you're walking!" I'd say. Then Shelton would snap at me, "Screw you!"

"No, screw you, man!" I'd shout back. Shelton would walk away, and I'd turn to the cashier and be like, "Man, what a jerk. This guy is walking around like he owns the store. You just can't treat people like that." And the cashier would always be on my side, like, "You're right. You can't treat people like that." We would go into it with words for so long, like at least five minutes, and that's a long time to argue in a convenience store in the middle of the night. And you could tell the cashier would be getting more and more freaked out, and then we'd do the big finish by taking it outside. The clerk never knew if he should call the cops or what.

The ultimate was when Shelton pulled up in the van, grabbed me, and threw me in like he was kidnapping me. We were laughing our asses off inside the van. We actually pulled this stunt about six or seven times, and it never got old. Sometimes we would even do it at a convenience store near an arena, so there would be a lot of fans hanging out there, and they would start to look at us like stuff was about to go down between Shelton and me for real. Everyone would be looking at us in shock like we really hated each other. Those were good times.

Two

Road Warriors

*"So not only did we just take a four-foot drop
in our rental car, but now we're locked in this
speaker store's parking lot."*

—JACK SWAGGER

**Think your back aches after a tough day on the job? Can't
wait to get out of rush-hour traffic just so you can get home
and relax? Now think about driving three hundred miles to a
show, getting suplexed a few times by a four-hundred-pound
opponent, then cramming back into a small rental car with
three or four other muscle-bound men as you drive three
hundred miles more to the next show. Now do that over two
hundred days a year. "The travel we do can be brutal at
times," Randy Orton tells me. "You figure a normal family
goes on vacation across the country and back over a week,
and that takes everything out of them to the point they almost**

need a vacation from their vacation. And they might only do that once a year. We live out of a suitcase. We live out of hotels and rental cars where three-hundred-mile drives are the norm. I'm around these guys more than I'm around my wife and my child. It's tough. We're a close-knit group of guys. Guys you can depend on and talk to and we're there for each other. Band of brothers . . . it really is."

With all that time on the road, the Superstars and Divas have gathered quite a collection of road trip stories. From late-night crashes in broken-down rentals to run-ins (and posing) with the police, you'll never view driving cross-country the same again.

Imagine driving down the freeway only to see Mark Henry lifting his car out of a ditch in the middle of the night . . .

World's Strongest Man . . .

No, Seriously

MVP

I was in a car one night with Mark Henry, and Mark was driving us to the airport. We end up going in the wrong direction, so Mark decides to make a U-turn, and

our car goes off the road a little bit and gets stuck in ice and snow. He kept hitting the gas, but our wheels were just spinning. We were stuck. We look at the clock, and time was really ticking down on us. If we didn't do something fast, we were going to miss our flight. So Mark told me to stay in the car, and when he gave me the word, I was supposed to hit the gas. I see Mark walk around to the back of the car, and next thing I know, he's actually lifting the back of the car up off the ground. And this wasn't a small car. We're talking about a Chevy Impala being lifted out of a ditch in the snow. The World's Strongest Man literally lifted the back end of our car so we could make our flight on time. I was so stunned, I didn't even have any words, and when he got back in the car, all he said was, "Man, I sure hope we don't miss our flight." The man didn't have to say anything else. He knew what needed to be done and he did it. His sheer strength just left me in awe. Mark Henry is better than a tow truck.

Strike a Pose

John Morrison

I call WWE an express train with very few stops. You get on the train and you usually don't get off until your career is over or you're injured. I got on this train in 2003 and I'm still on this train and everything that I've done and seen feels like a blur. It's like I just watched everything fly by at 100 miles per hour.

But when you're on the road, some crazy stuff just ends up happening. I remember this one time I was driving through Cleveland at about 110 miles per hour, or something ridiculously unsafe. And of course, I get pulled over by a cop. I was driving with Melina, and when the cop pulled me over he started yelling at me to get out of the car. I could tell by his voice that he was really nervous. He didn't have his gun drawn, but he must've thought I was some kind of drug dealer or criminal to be driving that fast. He's watching my every move, yelling at me to get out of the car. I roll the window down and put my hands out, and I yell to him, "I'm really sorry, sir. I'm just a WWE Superstar."

He's like, "What!?!"

So I told him again that I was a WWE Superstar, but he didn't understand what I was talking about, so I started to name-drop everyone from Hulk Hogan to Undertaker to The Rock. He looked at me and started shaking his head. "You don't look like one," he said.

So I was like, "Actually, I'm the Intercontinental Champion." But he still didn't believe me. That's when I told him I'd make him a deal. I told him that if he'd give me a break and not give me a ticket, I'd show him the championship belt. He looked at me, still not really believing me, but then he said, "Okay, if you show me your championship, I'll think about it."

And I swear, the second I took my championship belt out of my bag, he forgot all about being an officer and reverted back into little-kid mode. I handed him the belt, and he was holding it up like he had just won the title. Then he put it over his shoulder, and then he actually had me pose in front of his cop cam on his car where I was holding his hand up.

I don't think any of the boys would've ever believed this story if Viscera hadn't driven by right when I was holding the cop's hand up. The next day I was at the building trying to tell the story, and nobody believed me. They all thought it was BS. Five minutes later, Viscera walks in and was like, "Hey, Johnny, was that you standing on the side of the road just outside of Cleveland taking pictures with some cop and your belt?"

Everyone just looked at me, and I was like, "Yes, thank you. True that. That was me."

Just goes to show, it doesn't matter who you are, for some reason people see that championship and go nuts.

Mickie James

Life on the road is rough because if it's under three hundred miles to the next town, we're driving it. I remember there was a *Monday Night Raw* in Sioux Falls and I was driving back to Omaha because that's where we were flying out of the next morning. There was this huge blizzard, and they had shut down the roads for a while and weren't letting anyone drive. So they finally opened the roads, and I was riding with Katie Lea Burchill in this white Dodge Charger. Katie Lea is from Europe, and she was saying how she had never seen snow like this in Europe. So I start telling her, yeah, you need to be really careful because even though they cleaned the roads, there's still a lot of black ice out there. I was telling her how you could see the ice patches, but how the black ice isn't really something you could see. I'm sitting there explaining how you're supposed to navigate your way through black ice while I'm driving, and just as I tell her what you're supposed to do when you hit a patch of black ice, we hit a patch of black ice. I was like, "Oh no, oh no!" And we started to fishtail a little bit, but luckily I managed to steer the car straight. I was like, "Oh my God, that was a close one." As soon as I said that, the whole back end spun out and I started doing 360 after 360 after 360 after 360. We were in the middle of the highway with cars flying by us from both sides. In the middle of the road there was this huge median with a big ditch, and we had already done four 360s at least, and there we were in the median still spinning. The only way I can describe it is like we were living in a real-life snow globe because there was snow spinning all around us and there was nothing we could do about it. I'm fearing the worst, and when I look over, Katie is holding on for dear life. We both just kept screaming, "Make it stop, make it stop!"

Finally we stopped, and we were stuck in the middle of the median in this big ditch and we were packed in about three feet of snow. I get out of the car, and I'm not sure what to do, so I call the tow company, but they tell me that they can't come out and tow us because the police have just called all people off the road and the tow company needs to wait until the morning to find out if they get the all-clear. But that might not be until five or six in the morning. So I'm on the phone and I ask them, "So what am I supposed to do?" And they tell me that it's a $1,500 fine if they come out onto the road and help. But I'm outside in this blizzard and my car is stuck in a ditch, so I tell them, "I'll pay your fine if you come out." I had a flight to catch the next morning, and I just really wanted to make it to the hotel and get warm. But they told me, "Sorry, ma'am, we can't do that. It's against the law."

So I had Katie get behind the wheel, and I told her, "Okay, we're going to rock it. When I tell you to, gun it. Gun it, then let it off, gun it, then let it off." My job was to push the car while she gunned it, and I thought we could get the car back up the hill. Mind you, it is freakin' freezing outside, I'm in three and a half feet of snow, and coming from the show I'm still wearing what I wore on *Raw*, which is Diva clothing: not much to it and definitely not snow appropriate. I have my little leather jacket on and my Diva pants and I have the car rocking, but all that's happening is the tires are spinning and spitting dirty snow all over me. I'm frozen to the bone by that point, so I text John Cena and Beth Phoenix. I'm telling them how I'm stuck in this ditch and I don't know what to do. Luckily, they were both only a few minutes behind us on the same road, but by this point, literally, I saw my whole life flash in front of me while I was in this snow globe. My body was shaking, I was so freezing, and the only gloves I had were to keep me warm while I was walking from my car to the hotel—they weren't gloves to try to push a car out of a ditch during a blizzard.

But then I think we're saved because a cop in a truck pulls over before John or Beth even arrive. He calls me over, making me climb out of the ditch and walk all the way over to where he parked for some reason instead of getting out and walking toward us. Then he goes, "Ma'am, where do you think you're going?" So I tell him I already called the tow company but they wouldn't come out, and he goes, "Of course they're not going to come out. And ma'am, you can't be down there trying to push your car out of the ditch." So I ask him, "What am I supposed to do? I have a flight to catch in the morning." Then he tells me, "I can either take you to a hotel or you can come to the station and wait until the road is clear, but that won't be until five or six in the morning." But my flight was at seven, so I told him there was no way I could do that. So he asks me, "What do you want me to do then? Do you want me to take you to a hotel, or do you just want me to leave you here?" Next thing I know, he starts asking me if I'm the one who sideswiped some car. He's like, "Are you sure you didn't hit anybody?" And when I tell him no, he just goes, "Huh," and he leaves Katie and me there. He just drove off.

So there I was, walking back to the car and then trying to push it back up the hill again while Katie tried to gun it one last time. I still remember John finally pulling up and looking down at us after the cop had already left. He was like, "Get back in the car and warm up." Within a few minutes it ended up being John, Beth, Cody Rhodes, Ted DiBiase, and one of our security guys all out there trying to push my car out of this ditch. And I'll tell you how crazy John is, he was in sneakers and shorts, the shorts he wears to the ring, and a T-shirt. While the rest of us were trying to get bundled and wrapped up with as much as we can find, he's out there in a blizzard in his shorts.

Anyway, we all get behind the car and push it out of this ditch and back onto the road. Somehow, someway, we were able to all work together and get my car back on the road. So what we did was, we all followed each other the rest of the way to the hotel. We were this big trail of cars slowly working our way through the blizzard at 30 mph down the highway. Then we saw some guy who had also spun out up ahead, so we all pulled over and tried to get him out of the ditch as well. Then that same cop pulled up and told the guy that he had to leave his car there, so the guy hopped in someone's car and took off.

But all I kept thinking was, "Why would that cop just leave me there?" What if I was all alone? Would he have just left me to freeze? But looking back, we're just lucky there wasn't a whole lot of traffic on the road when we started to spin. Once we started into our 360s, I was just so worried that we were going to keep going all the way through the median to the other side and spin through the oncoming traffic. We're very fortunate that we ended up in the ditch, even if it did take us a long time to get out. Luckily, with the muscle of all our guys and the sheer brute strength of a couple of Divas, we were able to get out of there.

Wrestler's Rhapsody

Santino

One time we were on a long road trip. I was with Kennedy and Randy Orton, and they were both taking naps while I drove. Then that song "Bohemian Rhapsody" came on from Queen. I turned it up a little bit. I looked back and they were still sleeping, so I turned it up a little more. All of a sudden that part of the song comes on where it goes, "Figaro! Figaro!" and they both woke up and sang the different parts. Right from his sleep, Randy wakes up and sings, "Figaro! Figaro!" and Kennedy wakes up and sings, "Galileo! Galileo!" It was too funny. It was like a real-life *Wayne's World* moment.

Hungry Man

Mark Henry

As far as the camaraderie and enjoying the journey, life on the road is good. But being a big guy, it's hard to maneuver around hotels, flights, and small rental cars. It's difficult.

One of the funniest things that happened was the night Tony Atlas and I were in a car after a show in Monroe, Louisiana, and as we were driving, I kept telling him that I was hungry and that we needed to pull over and get something to eat. But Tony kept saying we'd stop later, even though I told him over and over that I wanted to eat. Next thing we know, the tire on our car popped and we're stuck on the side of the road. But the rental car agency, they didn't put all of the tools to fix the tires in the trunk. So we called Avis and started fussing at them, and in the meantime I'm cussing Tony out because I'm hungry, I'm stuck on the side of the road, and because he never pulled over I have no food.

So I call Justin, our announcer, and I tell him what happened, how we called Avis and they're sending someone out to repair our tire, and I tell him that if he passes a Subway or something, that he should bring me a sandwich. So Justin actually finds a Subway that's still open, and he buys me a sandwich and brings it to me before they come fix our tire. So there I am, sitting on the trunk of the car eating my sandwich as traffic flies by. I'm just hoping I don't get hit, but I don't care, all I wanted to do was eat at that point.

Tony was sitting in the car because he was scared. All he kept saying was, "There are snakes out there. I don't want to get bit by no snakes." I told him, "C'mon, man, there aren't any snakes on the highway." So now Jesse and Festus pull up, and they have the same kind of car we rented, so we go into their trunk, pull out the tools, and start fixing our tire. Next thing we know, Tony jumps out of the car to help, but he doesn't have the car in park. When he was in the car his foot was on the brake, but now he jumps out, taking his foot off the brake, and Jesse was underneath the car changing the tire. The new tire wasn't even on yet and now the car starts rolling back. Everyone was like, "Oh no!" Jesse gets pulled back out of the way— he almost got crushed by the car. That's not the funny part. We were all like, "Damn, Tony, why didn't you put the car in park?" And he said, "Why does everybody always try to blame everything on me? Awww!"

So now they go back to fixing the tire, but we were

right on the edge of the road, and I'm standing there making sure no car gets close to hitting us. By that time the roadside assistance guy calls and says he's lost. We told him exactly where we were at, the highway, the mile marker, and everything. So I told him, "We got the car fixed now, so you can just turn around and go back." This was an hour and a half after we initially called. And the guy goes, "If you don't mind, I'm going to tell Avis that I helped you so I can get paid." I was like, "I mind."

After the tire is fixed, Tony tells me that we should drive to Nashville . . . that was like four and a half hours away! I told him, "There's no way in hell I'm riding on this donut for the next four and a half hours." He tells me, "Well, if we go fifty miles per hour, we'll be fine." And I'm like, "Tony, it's going to take us six or seven hours to get to Nashville on a donut, with a good chance we're going to end up popping the donut and be on the side of the road once again." I told him we'd stop in Birmingham, change cars, call the office, and tell them that we might be late for the show. We'd get there when we get there. Tony started panicking. He wasn't used to calling the office and dealing with problems. He was used to dealing with problems his own way, but that's another story. I still just remember Tony sitting there mad, saying, "We're stuck on the side of the road and you worried about eating." I was like, "That's because you didn't work today." What can I say, I wanted a sandwich.

Jumping the Wrong Curb

Jack Swagger

The road: That's where you really earn everything that's thrown at you. The travel schedule is crazy. Once you get into it, three months seems like a year because you're working every weekend. There are a lot of good times too, because we have a good group of guys, a really good atmosphere backstage, so to travel with these guys, they really become your family. The three-hundred-mile drives can be tough, but it's worth it.

Strange things end up happening, though, when you spend so much time driving. A few months ago, we were in Laredo, Texas, trying to get to this Outback Steakhouse. I'm driving down the street and all of a sudden it turns into a one-way street heading into this hotel. But instead of pulling all the way around to get to the Outback, I think I can cut through the hotel parking lot, but as I pull around, I see that the parking lot is all blocked in. So I'm driving around and I see this little area open up, and it looks like a little service road, so I figure I'll just drive down off what looked like a little curb and we'll be right there. Only thing is, as I'm driving out of the parking lot and onto the grass in front of this curb, I realize the drop is actually about four feet down, right onto cement. So I try to stop, but I hit the brakes too late and we can't stop and the front wheels are off the curb. I try to back up, but the tires are just spinning, so the only place I can go now is down. So I take the rental car and we do the drop. *Bam!* Not too much damage, just messed up the bumper a little bit. But now we realize we're not even in the Outback parking lot. We just dropped into the parking lot of some speaker store, and not only is the store closed, they have their parking lot gated off and the gate is locked. So not only did we just take a four-foot drop in our rental car, but now we're locked in this speaker store's parking lot.

So we're looking around and we find some little wooden pallets, and there we are in the middle of the night, trying to build a bridge back up the four-foot drop so we can drive back to our original spot by the hotel. Unfortunately, all we end up doing is messing the car up some more. Next thing we know, a cop pulls up and he's just looking at us, like, "What do you guys think you're doing?" Luckily for us, the cop ended up calling the owner, and the owner of the speaker store came down and unlocked the gate for us. The whole time, though, the cop just kept looking at us like we were idiots.

Full Moon

Maria

I like to drive fast. Very, very fast. And this one time I was driving fast, and of course I get pulled over, but what I didn't realize is that I had another speeding ticket that I forgot to take care of. So I'm driving by myself in the middle of Ohio, there's nobody around for miles, and I'm going about eighty-five to ninety in a sixty-five-mile-per-hour zone. When the cop pulls me over, he tells me, "I can't let you drive. You don't have a valid license." I was like, "What?" I didn't realize that I had this other speeding ticket out, so they ended up towing my car and I was stuck on the side of the road with all of my suitcases waiting for a cab to come pick me up. All of a sudden, this other car goes zooming by and my phone starts ringing. It's Matt Hardy, and he's like, "Are you on the side of the road?"

I started telling him what happened, how I don't have a car, and he ends up pulling around, and he's with his brother Jeff, and they pick me up and bring me to the show.

They always tell me they're my angels now because they picked me up from the side of the road. It was absolutely ridiculous, but yes, this really happened to me.

The other thing that happens a lot on the road is people mooning each other. Of course, I can't name names on that one, but we like to entertain ourselves with that.

And of course, it's always an adventure driving with Maryse because she doesn't know where anything is inside the car. I even have to tell her where the blinker is. I remember this one time we were driving through some town and we decided to stop at a Starbucks. We figure there are so many places to stop that we wouldn't see anyone, so we get our coffee and hop back in the car. But when Maryse goes to pull out, she somehow hops up on a curb, and for like two minutes we're seriously driving over this big curb in front of Starbucks. We just laugh it off and think it's no big deal because nobody was around to see what was happening, but then when we get to the show, Fit Finlay was like, "Was that you guys?" He had seen us driving over the curb laughing our butts off and not even caring. We figured that between shows was about three hundred miles, no way anyone saw that. But it's always that way. We always end up stopping at the same gas stations, the same places to go to the bathroom, the same food places. For some reason, everyone always stops at the same places.

Tennessee, Part 1

Shad

My most messed-up road story is the time Jay and I were driving through Tennessee. We left our hotel and started driving, but when we were on the road, some guy in his minivan, driving his family, he cut us off. And so me, being a New Yorker, I sped up and got ahead of him and cut him off back, then just kept driving. A couple of miles up the road, a cop came flying up on us, got in front of us, and pulled us over. First thing he asked us is if we had drugs in the car. I told him we didn't have any drugs. Then he wanted to see my license and registration, and I said, "Cool." I tell him it's a rental car, then I reach over to grab my license and the cop rips the door open. He pulls out his Taser gun and points it at me, telling me to get out of the car. I didn't want to get out, but he said he was going to Tase me if I didn't get out, so I got out. When I stand up, I'm 6'7", this guy is 5'8" and he's an old, fat, hillbilly cop. Next thing I know I'm in handcuffs and the cops are telling me how they know we're drug dealers and how they just know we're transporting drugs over state lines. I'm like, "Really?" Then all of a sudden, there are like six more cop cars pulling up along with a drug dog. The dog goes in and starts sniffing the car, and the only thing they find is some weed residue that must've just been left over from the rental car. I'm telling him it's a rental car, that we don't have any drugs, and that the residue is not from us . . . it's a damn rental, but he tells me that he's taking me to jail.

To make things worse, we had an autograph signing that we needed to get to and it was two hours away. So I'm sitting in the back of the cop car, and we're on our way to jail, and I tell the cop, "You know why you're doing this, right?" And he's like, "Why?" So I tell him, "It's because I'm black." The cop was like, "No, you were breaking the law." So I asked him, "What law was I breaking?" And he tells me I was speeding. After all that, he was taking me in for speeding. I was going like two miles an hour over the speed limit and they were arresting me! So I kept talking. I told him how he screwed up. How he put me in handcuffs in front of everyone, so he had to arrest me even if I didn't do anything. This guy argued with me the entire way to the police station. We finally pull up, they close the gate, and this guy tells me I have two choices: I can either wait until Monday and go to court, or if I give him one hundred dollars, he'd let me go right there. So of course, I gave him a hundred dollars, and on the hundred-dollar bill I wrote "F--- you!" I walked out of there a free man.

The funny thing about it was, one of the other cops told me that they were informed of two black guys running drugs by the minivan we cut off. Turns out the guy driving the minivan was an off-duty officer. The cop in the minivan called it in saying we were smoking blunts as we were driving down the road. I told them I don't smoke weed. I've never failed a drug test. The cop told me that once they got on the crime scene with the drug dog, they knew we were clean. They knew the residue was from the rental car and not from us. And they also knew who we were. Last thing he said was, "Can I get your autograph?"

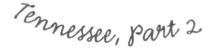

Tennessee, part 2

JTG

There are some good times in Tennessee. It's not just all about what Shad said.

One night we ran out of gas and we had to pull over to the side of the road. We had seen a gas station, but it was miles away. Shad wanted to hike there, but I was like, "Hey man, I'm rockin' Timbs here, I'm not hiking to no gas station."

So I stuck my leg out and some ladies pulled over. We didn't get to the gas station right away, but we had some fun on the way there, ya dig?

The other thing we love to do is roast each other in the car. Me, Shad, and Kofi go at it nonstop. I love to roast. We love to make it hot. Just thinking about it makes me hot. That's how I get my kicks, that's my passion, roasting Kofi. I'll roast him right now, that fake Jamaican. I call him a Jafakin'. I love Kofi though, that's my boy. But we roast each other from sunup to sundown. It can be three, four in the morning and it's still just continuous roast. Then when one of us does something good and we start to compliment each other, we get right back to cutting each other down. We cut each other right back down to reality. Like, "Hey, that was a nice match . . . but you're still bad."

Was That Flying Hummus?

Dolph Ziggler

I'm a boring guy. Life on the road for me is usually gym-hotel-sleep–wrestling show . . . gym-hotel-sleep–wrestling show. There was this one time, though, where we saw Gail Kim driving in the car next to us, so naturally we started throwing plastic bottles at her car. After a couple of the plastic bottles hit her car, and we naturally went back and recycled them, we all stopped up the road and had a good laugh while we got gas. Next thing we knew, Gail Kim and Alicia Fox came out of the convenience store and pelted us with powdered donuts. We all thought, "Oh how funny, everything is now even and fair." But then as I was about to open my car door, Gail Kim took a bowl of hummus and threw it over the roof of her car and winged it at me. I just happened to be turning to look at something at the same time for some reason, so I saw it out of the corner of my eye and managed to avoid it. The flying hummus grazed my hair and splattered all over the car behind me. Gail Kim is here and alive right now, so that is testament that she never hit me. But hummus at a gas station? I didn't even know you could do that. A sandwich maybe, but hummus?

Usually when you have a really good car ride, though, you're not distracted by flying food or bottles. If you're having a real good car ride, you don't ever turn the radio on. I've been traveling with Tommy Dreamer and Christian for a little while now, and I don't know that we ever turn on the radio. Here are a couple of guys who have been around, been to the top, and are still at the top of their games. So it helps me out riding along with them.

They are really helping me become a better Superstar. One thing they stress to me is how some people have a couple thousand matches, and you're going to have a bad night somewhere along the road. Sometimes you have maybe twelve hours to think about it before your next match, and you need to use that time to figure out what your mistakes were and let it go. You need to move on to the next match and do better next time. Almost like a quarterback in football: You get picked off, you have to lead your team right back down the field and score a touchdown. It's hard to let those bad matches go, but you need to move on if you want to move up.

Look Ma, No Hands

Santino

Randy Orton likes to mess with me while I'm driving all the time. He'll check my blind spot, and if no one is beside me, he'll grab the wheel and change lanes on me really fast without saying anything. It just got to the point where now when I see him grab the wheel, I try to get him back a little by taking my hands completely off the wheel while he's turning. I'm like, "Go ahead and take it." I know he's not going to make us smash.

Turning Heads

Ezekiel Jackson

I'm used to being the big guy, but then I started traveling with Khali. So I'm walking into places, and now people are looking at me wondering who is this small guy talking to the really big guy. I remember walking into a Denny's with Khali in Alabama. Everyone stopped what they were doing and gave us one of those "holy crap" moments. Here I am, I'm not a small person, but I'm walking into Denny's in Alabama with a giant. You can imagine the faces of everyone inside. You don't even get comments from people, they're just speechless.

No matter where we go to eat, though, it's always funny to see the looks on people's faces. Here I am, a 6'4", 300-pound dude with muscles bulging from everywhere. Then you have a 7'4", 400-something-pounder walking in. It's like, "Holy crap!" What else can you even say? You just see them look, then there are a lot of whispers around the tables. That's life on the road for me and Khali.

Unfortunately, when we do travel, everybody still thinks I'm Bobby Lashley. I've been called Bobby Lashley, I've been called Ahmed Johnson . . . but I'm Ezekiel Jackson. If you don't recognize me, that's cool, but don't get mad at me if I don't sign. I'm not going to sign Bobby Lashley's name.

Christian

In my car, it's usually me, Edge, and Tommy Dreamer. Then when Edge got hurt, Dolph Ziggler jumped in with us, and in our car it's nonstop talking. We talk about everything and anything from wrestling to sports to politics to finance. There are a lot of different things going on in our car, a lot of good debate. What's great for me is the invention of the iPhone, because so many times there are disputes about who is right and who is wrong during these talks, so I just jump on my iPhone and use Google or Wikipedia to figure out 99.9 percent of the time that I'm right. We always seem to argue over which actor appeared in a certain movie or which band played a certain song. The iPhone makes it so easy to end an argument.

iDisagree

Tommy Dreamer

Christian is never always right. That's just Christian's ego talking there, but he is the master of everything iPhone. He looks up anything and everything that we might have a question about. It's pretty funny because it could be the most random question about the drummer of some band we hear on the radio, and he looks up everything he can on the guy and then informs us. He's like a human *Pop-Up Video* guy.

But when it comes to traveling, I don't think fans realize just how much we're actually on the road. On the ECW / *SmackDown!* side, we usually work Saturday, Sunday, Monday, then we do TV on Tuesday. They'll fly us from our home to wherever our first destination is, then we usually get into a rental car and drive anywhere up to three hundred miles. It's just what we do. We spend a lot of hours in hotel rooms and inside cars. But this time inside the car, it's so important because this is where you learn by talking to some of the veterans who you share rides with. Wrestling isn't just about living your dream and having fun. This is a business, and we talk about any variety of topics just to keep awake, from current events to your future, to what's going on with your career. A lot of younger guys don't realize that it's hard to find that longevity in this business. I'm sure Christian can Google name after name of guys who have come and gone in this business using his iPhone. Guys who didn't know anything about the importance of financial planning or trying to build for their future. That's the kind of stuff you learn in the car. If you're a young guy just starting out, the most important thing you could do for your career is to ride with a couple of veterans so you can learn about this business the right way.

Measuring Up

Evan Bourne

One time I was traveling with Colin Delaney and we had just gotten on the road. We were the super rookies at this point, and we were riding with another guy named "Cadillac" Casey James, who was a developmental guy who never really made it on TV. But while we were driving, we all started having this debate: How long are the white stripes in the middle of the road? Blazing down the highway, they look like they're only three or four feet, but

Cadillac says, "No, they're ten feet long. I swear to you, they're ten to twelve feet long." Me and Colin are like, "Hell no. At max these things are six feet, but the lines are not taller than us. These lines are not longer than me." So we end up pulling over into a Whataburger parking lot and go out to the street to stand out there on the lines and measure foot to foot, toe to toe. And I'll be darned, these white lines in the middle of the road really were twelve feet. We were dead wrong. So here we are, Colin and I are in the middle of the street at like one in the morning, walking a tightrope along these lines to measure, when we see another car pull into Whataburger. They turn right by us, and it's Teddy Long and Mark Henry. They both just looked at us, they looked at each other, and Teddy was like, "What are you boys doing out there in the middle of the street?" It was definitely a shocking experience for them to see us out there, but we had to know who was right about those lines. I still can't believe they're twelve feet.

That's the Jam

MVP

My musical tastes are real eclectic. I listen to a lot of hip-hop and jazz. I'm really into Jamiroquai, Paul Wall, Led

Zeppelin, Young Jeezy . . . depends on my mood. I had Chris Masters in the car with me a while back, and as we're driving along we were listening to jazz for a while. And this was classic jazz . . . a trio with the drummer, pianist, and a trumpet. I love jazz, especially the classic stuff with Charlie Parker, and after about five or ten minutes, Chris Masters turns to me and is like, "Man, this is really cool." He had never really listened to jazz like that before. After a while, the song is over and there's a commercial on the station, so I change it, and Living Colour is on with "Cult of Personality." He had never heard that song before. Then when I told him they were black, I blew him away. He was like, "For real?" A couple of minutes later, Fleetwood Mac came on with "The Chain," and he had never heard that either. I think by the time we had finished our drive, I had enlightened him and broadened his musical horizons. Everyone always looks at me and thinks, "MVP: hip-hop, rap, and that ballin' Superstar," but musically, my tastes are all over the place. I like what I like. I can talk music for hours.

The All-American American's Ultimate Road Hit List

Jack Swagger

One thing people don't know about me is, I love to sing. That doesn't mean I'm a good singer—in fact, I'm a horrible singer—but I love doing it. And while I love music, I have absolutely no musical ability whatsoever. It's funny because every once in a while I'll be jamming out and I'll catch a strange look from somebody I'm riding with, like, "Dude, c'mon, let's wrap this up."

Anyway, here are five of my favorite artists to drive to and sing along with (to the dismay of everyone else in the car) . . .

5. **Madonna, "Like a Prayer": You gotta have a little something for everyone, and you never know when you'll be traveling with a Diva.**

4. **Billy Idol, "Rebel Yell": I just love Billy Idol, and this song gets me pumped up. Every trip needs a song like this to get your heart really pumping.**

3. **Taking Back Sunday: One of my favorite bands. It's hard to pick one song, so just put all their CDs on your iPod before a trip.**

2. **Kings of Leon: Everything Kings of Leon does is great. They're from Oklahoma and are big Oklahoma Sooner fans.**

1. **Dr. Dre, "Let Me Ride": Talk about a song that makes me sing. This is my favorite hip-hop song of all time. [*Starts singing*] "Let me ride . . ."**

Million Dollar U-Turn

IRS

Back in the early nineties, Ted DiBiase and I were tag team partners and our team was known as Money Inc. I remember going down the New York State Thruway, we were on the toll road and it had to be about two or three in the morning, so there was no traffic on the road. There was snowy weather, and it was getting pretty nasty out there, and as we're driving along, driving along, we miss our exit. So we keep driving, but then we see the sign that the next exit isn't for thirty miles. So Ted goes, "We're just going to have to turn around in the middle of the thru-way." We hadn't seen another car in probably twenty to thirty minutes, so he sees a spot to make a U-turn, and we turn around in the middle of the thruway and start heading back in the opposite direction. Sure enough, five minutes later, we see the blue lights, and a patrol car was pulling us over from behind. It was just one of those deals we couldn't believe. Here we were, driving for twenty to thirty minutes without seeing another car, then as soon as we do something we shouldn't, the cops show up. Why does it always seem to happen like that?

Tyson Kidd

Driving from Tampa to Miami, it's myself, Natalya, and David Hart, and there was a sign that said "Last Stop for Gas." I had about a quarter of a tank left, but it said that the next gas was in eighty miles. I figured I could make eighty miles easy. And this way, if we didn't stop, we would've gotten to Miami by eight o'clock the night before the show. So we're driving, and Natalya of course says, "I don't know, I think you should stop for gas." But I assure her, "No, no, it's fine." Long story short, we ran out of gas.

I kept seeing it was low, and I was watching the miles on the car, and when we got to about seventy-eight miles, we were out. And there were no service stations anywhere. DH was sleeping, Nattie was half asleep and not really paying attention, so I kept punching in searches for service stations on the GPS, and the GPS is now telling me the closest is twenty-four miles away. I'm like, "Oh no!" Now, I'm pretty stubborn, so what's even worse for me than running out of gas is me being wrong. I just kept saying, "No, no, we gotta get there. We gotta get there." Well, next thing we know, we lose the power, and I start to pull over to the side of the road. Natalya looks at me and says, "You ran out of gas, right?" And I had to tell her, "Yep, we ran out of gas."

So now we're on the side of the road in the middle of nowhere and there's nothing around but highways. But I knew there were a few other guys driving in from Tampa, so I call Tyler Reks because I knew he was one of them. We were only half an hour outside of Miami, and luckily for us, Tyler Reks was only about forty-five minutes behind us. But as we waited for him to show up, Natalya and David walked down the road trying to find one of those emergency phones. While they were walking, some lady pulls over and offers to give them a ride to a gas station, so they tell me to stay with the car. So I stay with the car and after a while, Tyler shows up. Luckily, he tells me he'll wait with me until they show up with the gas. Now, I'm assuming that this lady is bringing them back. But then Natalya calls me and says, "The lady just dropped us off." She pulled up to some random gas station and told them to get out and drove off. So now they're stuck at some gas station that we don't even know where it is, and I'm stuck with my car—this wasn't even a rental car—and I'm stuck there with Tyler Reks and the guys riding with him. So I jump in their car to go get some gas in a jerry can, drive back to my car to fill it up, and by this time it's already after ten thirty. Now I'm filling up the car and gas is spilling out all over the place. Natalya had just bought me a pair of brand-new Puma shoes for my birthday, and when I get to the hotel at eleven thirty at night, I realize that my shoes are completely ruined from the gasoline. All because I tried to drive with no gas. It was a long, long, long, long drive to Miami that night. Then I went on to wrestle Cryme Tyme twice the next night, and that's even worse than the drive.

The Bicker Twins

Nikki Bella

One time Brie and I were driving through Reno, and we love to sing and dance in the car, and we were blasting songs from the eighties. I had an open water bottle and some of it got on Brie while I was dancing, so she turned around and poured her whole water bottle on me. All of a sudden, I'm dumping the rest of my water bottle on her, and we got into this full-on water fight while we were driving. By the time we made it to the gas station to fill up, we were both dripping wet and it was freezing cold. We were already in our Diva outfits, lace and heels, so we had people staring at us. Here we are, twin Divas walking up to the gas station attendant dripping wet on a cold night. He was just staring at us, like, "What the hell is happening?"

But Brie and I always fight when we're on the road. We're like husband and wife the way we bicker the entire time. That's why people like The Miz like to travel with us. I remember this one time I had the GPS in my hand and Brie was driving. So she asked me, "What am I going to make?" And I told her, "Make a right." Two seconds later, she's like, "Wait, what am I going to make?" And I tell her

again, "You're going to make a right." Two seconds later, I swear, she asks me again, so I start yelling, "YOU'RE GOING TO MAKE A RIGHT!" And what does she do? She makes a freakin' left! I was like, "Bri-anna!" and I just started yelling. So now The Miz, all the time he walks up to us with this voice that he does and says, "Bri-anna! No way! Just shut up, just shut up." He does all these impressions of us all the time, and it's all because Brie doesn't know her rights from her lefts.

Living "The Life"

Cody Rhodes

Three in the morning, can't sleep, sometimes you have those long, three-hundred-mile drives and you're on the road at all hours of the night. One game we like to play is with the iPod receivers inside the car. We call it "The Life" game, where you turn the radio all the way down and one person shuffles the iPod until someone shouts stop. When someone says stop, you turn the radio up and whatever song that is playing, that is the song that describes your life for that day. It's always funny. The last time for me, I turned it down and as I cranked it up, the song was "You Belong with Me," by Taylor Swift. So it had no actual reference to my life, but it was my Life song for the day.

This is a game that Ted DiBiase, Randy Orton, Beth Phoenix, Santino Marella, and I like to play. I think the best of the best is when Randy got an instrumental once. We were all like, "Uh-oh, that's the most ominous song that could play." It was so ambiguous, no lyrics or anything . . . it was just an instrumental for Randy Orton. But the way he played it, he said luck was on his side. Since there weren't any lyrics, you could make it anything, and he flipped it into a positive. But for me, keep me away from those instrumentals. I'll take Taylor Swift for my Life song any day.

But getting back to those long drives, one thing that should be established as a major faux pas of road tripping is, don't be a phone-talker. Do not get on the phone with your wife, your girlfriend, or your buddy and talk for thirty minutes. That means the music in the car needs to be turned down when you're on the phone, conversations in the car can't take place, and it makes the trip seem that much longer.

Ted DiBiase is a notorious phone-talker, and that is the worst. And he's never talking to anyone important. It's Jimmy from Iowa who he met at church when they were eleven, and they'll talk for half an hour. Never anyone important. Never.

No Driver Necessary

Goldust

What people don't realize is that us wrestlers are professionals when it comes to stunt driving.

I remember a long time ago I was driving from Fort Lauderdale back to Tampa and I was trying to catch up to Barry Windham. Barry was my mentor. He was in a car up ahead of me, and I was driving by myself in a big Lincoln Continental. So I'm driving and I see his car, then I slide over into the passenger side while keeping my left foot on the pedal and holding the steering wheel with my left knee. I'm going like eighty-five to ninety miles per hour, and I'm leaning my head against the passenger-side window with a newspaper in my hand while I pass him. I'm looking at the newspaper while trying to watch the road at the same time, and when I pull up beside him, Barry gave a double take because he couldn't figure out who was driving the car. You had to see his face to believe it. It was really cool. I used to do that all the time and I always loved it. It used to freak people out. They'd be like, "If Dustin's reading the paper, who is driving his car?"

The DibiDot

Beth Phoenix

In the attempt to entertain ourselves, we've gotten into the habit of raiding local gas stations for the most bizarre items we could find. It's all about buying the most random stuff we could find at gas stations and rest stops. I don't know where or how they got this, but Ted and Cody bought this rubber Koosh ball that looked like a dot with little eyes on it and some little rubber hair sticking out of the top. If you poke or punch this thing, a light starts to flash in the middle. So they hung this ball from the rearview mirror for this long loop we had, from Friday to Monday night, and it got lovingly named the DibiDot. It was in reference to DiBiase, and I don't know why, but this strange rubber Koosh with little eyes and hair sticking up became the DibiDot. So then each weekend after that, we were on a mission to find more of these Koosh balls to hang from our mirror. But there were times when we bought cowboy hats and the weird Hawaiian bobble-head ladies for the dashboard, and maybe a pirate's hat on one side and a buccaneer's hat on the other. I remember this one time we found a Jeff Gordon air freshener. That was my favorite, because Jeff Gordon had this really strange look on his face and it was quite an interesting smell. And when we looked on the package, it didn't even say what the smell was supposed to be, so I was like, "Hey, this smells like Jeff Gordon."

That's Not All We Buy

Ted DiBiase

Actually, when it comes to buying the most random item from a gas station or a truck stop, John Cena is the best. We'll go to these huge truck stops where all the truckers stop and sleep, and you can find the strangest things you could ever imagine. Cena bought this massive Elvis painting one time, and we just put it in the front window of our rental car the rest of the weekend as we drove. We buy cowboy hats, Koosh balls . . . if it's weird and they sell it, we're buying. What's funny is when you go to return the car to the rental agency and you just leave all of that stuff in there. One time I would love to see the reaction of the guy who has to clean our car out. I wonder what they do with Elvis paintings and piles of McDonald's bags.

Big Show

I was so sick of all the problems associated with traveling that I went out and got a tour bus. You see, Big Show now rides around in a million-and-a-half-dollar tour bus with a driver. But the young Big Show, that was a different story. The young Big Show one time had a Tuesday-night TV taping in Rome, Georgia, but I had an 11:20 P.M. flight out of the Atlanta airport that I wanted to make. Now, Rome, Georgia, is about an hour and twenty minutes away from Atlanta on a normal drive, and we had to go through Atlanta to the other side to make the airport. But like I said, I really wanted to make my flight. "Mean" Gene Okerlund lived in Tampa as well and was also on my flight, so he wanted to catch a ride with me to the airport. I said, "Sure, Gene, no problem." But then we wrapped up from TV a little late, and Gene didn't think we'd be able to make it to the airport on time.

Now, back then, we used to rent Cadillac DeVilles, and those Cadillac DeVilles, their speedometers shut down at 112 mph. So I set the cruise control at 110 mph and headed to the airport. We go through Atlanta, stop at the Omni hotel in downtown Atlanta so Gene could grab his suit bag from the concierge. The bellman handed it to Gene as he jumped out, then he hopped back in the car and we hauled ass through Atlanta and got to the airport with enough time to drop off our rental car at the Avis return. We made it from Rome, Georgia, to the Atlanta airport in fifty-eight minutes with a stop in Atlanta to pick up the suit.

"Mean" Gene never said a word the entire trip. We go through check-in, get on the plane, and we're sitting next to each other when "Mean" Gene orders two drinks back to back. He slammed them both and looked as white as a sheet. He looked right at me and said, "Well, if I ever need to get somewhere in a hurry, I know who to call."

I never even thought anything about it. I was just trying to make our flight. But I guess I completely terrified "Mean" Gene Okerlund and took a few years off of his life with that one car ride.

These days, though, like I said, different story. I ride in Toby Keith's "American Soldier" bus, and I have a driver to take me wherever I need to go. The bus has a big king-size bed in the back, fifty-inch plasmas, Michelob Ultra Light on tap, Bud Light on tap, full bar . . . I don't even drink that much, but every now and then, it's great to have a cold beer. I've got wireless Internet, DIRECTV, and I even have an Xbox 360 hooked up so I can play all of my first-person shooters, like *Rainbow Six: Vegas, Call of Duty*, and *Wolfenstein.*

I like it because I never have to look for hotel rooms. I always have a locker room to get dressed in, I always have my own shower, and since I have all of my clothes in the back, if I need a suit or something special to wear, I have it with me accessible at all times. About the only bag I bring with me to the airport is the one holding my computer and my wallet. That's about it. So these days, in the States, traveling works out really well thanks to the bus.

Driving up and down the road two hundred and fifty to three hundred miles every night, I did it for twelve years and it's just too much for me. So the past couple of years I've been on my bus and it works out so much better. I'm done with hotels. I'm done checking into hotels at three in the morning. You wouldn't believe how many times I've checked into a hotel, they see how big I am, but then they give me a room with two double beds. Give me a break.

Something Everyone Should Strive For

Randy Orton

Show, Hunter, and Taker all have these tour buses that they travel on, and now that Hunter is getting a new bus custom built, I'm taking his old bus off his hands. So many guys don't realize how great these buses are. Stone Cold, The Rock . . . these guys never did it. I think Hunter was the first one to do it, and it costs some money, but in the long run, we pay for our own rental cars and hotel already. That's not taken care of. It's a write-off for us, but we spend hundreds of thousands of dollars on rental cars and hotel stays each year, and that cost will be erased by having the bus. Sure, the bus is a little more, but the benefits are unbelievable. Now when I fly into a town, that bus picks me up and I don't need to worry about a rental car. My driver will take me to go eat, and inside the bus I have a fridge, an oven, a microwave, a washer, a dryer, bathroom, shower, king-size bed, a crew bunk, a bed for my baby with a crib, and even a little lounging area with two flatscreens. It's like a traveling apartment.

So while I'm at the show, my driver can leave and go pick up some Outback or something to eat at the grocery store and make sure I have something for dinner. After my match, instead of hitting the showers in the locker room, getting dressed, and going out in the rental car and finding something to eat, a process that can take up to two hours before we even start our three-hundred-mile drive to the next town, now I can just go straight on the bus, eat dinner, and shower. And by the time I'm showered up, I've already eaten, and now I'm relaxing and playing video games on the bus or watching TV or sleeping, and we're already in the next town . . . or at least halfway there. Then I get better sleep. And to top it off, I'm not sitting in the front seat of the car for hundreds of miles, which is horrible for your back, especially with what we do. I'm able to lie down, relax, and I can even bring my wife and child whenever I want.

As far as overall health, longevity, and stress level, it's night and day. The bus gives you so much more opportunity, so much more time. Without the bus, you're driving in the middle of the night, maybe get to your hotel at four o'clock, then you wake up at one in the afternoon, head to the gym, and it's always rush-rush-rush-rush-rush just to make it to the next show. With that bus, I'll be able to sleep and get up at a decent time and still be able to get my stuff done.

When I started, it was still like three or four years until GPS was around. But now having a driver and not even thinking about being behind the wheel and being able to sleep on the road, that's as good as it gets. That should be the ultimate goal for any of us. Where you can get to a position in the company where you can afford the luxury of the bus. The bar has been raised to this. Now you know, if you can afford this type of luxury, you've made it. You're finally where you want to be.

Three

Time to Play
the Game

"You know how embarrassing that is? A person who

doesn't even play that much to beat someone

who plays every day?"

—THE MIZ

Back in the Nation days, Mark Henry once lost his European

Championship to The Rock in a backstage game of *Madden.*

Henry destroyed The Rock in the rematch and eventually

took his title back with him to *Raw,* but this story just goes to

show how invested some of these athletes are in their video

games. ✪ In fact, Christian was once one of the top-rated

online players at a tennis game called *Top Spin 2.* "I figured

I'd play the game until I was ranked number one in the

world," he tells me, "then I could break the disk and never

play it again." Didn't happen. Instead, Christian ended up losing to some guy from England after his opponent kept hitting lob shot after lob shot, frustrating the wrestler and throwing him off his game. "So afterward, I'm asking the guy why he did that and we end up getting into an argument over the headsets," Christian explains. "Next thing I know the door to my game room swings open and my wife is standing there with her hands on her hips, glaring at me like a mother scolding a child."

And while that might have been Christian's last game of *Top Spin 2*, the video game competitions across the WWE roster continue to heat up, especially in a car full of *Madden* gamers as they play round-robin tournaments while they travel the world.

Who is the champ? Depends on who you ask.

Evan Bourne

I usually drive the car when I travel with Kofi Kingston, Hornswoggle, and The Miz, and those three have a heated *Madden* rivalry. There's so much smack talk going on, I can literally hear them shouting things like, "March, march, march, march, I'm marching down the field," while they play. I'll ask for score updates while I drive, but sometimes I actually need to referee these guys because they are getting really upset at each other. When Miz starts losing, he gets very upset. And whenever Hornswoggle wins, he just grinds that victory in. He digs it in and keeps reminding Miz who beat him, and he will ask about the score for the rest of the night. Just digging and digging it in. I would say the most fun I have is riding in that car with Hornswoggle, Miz, and Kofi when they're playing that game.

The Underdog

Hornswoggle

When we're on the road, Kofi and I constantly play *Madden*. We have a big video game rivalry, and a big rivalry in general about everything. It's a friendly rivalry, and we play jokes on each other constantly. He makes fun of my love for the Muppets, and I make fun of his love for just about everything else. But when it comes to *Madden*, nobody can beat me.

Things can get pretty heated in the car when we play, though, especially between Kofi and Miz. One time they made a bet that if Miz won, Miz would autograph Kofi's PSP. But if Kofi won, he would sign Miz's stupid guitar that

we all hate but he demands to bring everywhere we go. Kofi ended up killing him and immediately pulled out his pen. I even took a picture of the victory celebration using my iPhone. So now every time Miz wants to play his guitar, he's staring at Kofi's signature. Priceless.

The Miz

When I travel with Kofi Kingston and Hornswoggle, we always end up having these long video game feuds. One of us will drive while the other two are playing video games on the PSP. Now, Hornswoggle and Kofi are avid *Madden* players. Huge, huge fans of the game, and the thing about it is, I'll play here and there. I play sporadically, and really, the only time I ever play is when I'm in the car playing against them. I don't play anywhere else. But I beat them almost half the time we play, and these guys play every single day. They go online and play *Madden* all the time with their little headsets, like, "Ohhhh, I'm going to beat you, I'm going to beat you." They're doing that whole thing all the time, and here I am with my little PSP portable player, and I'm beating them. You know how embarrassing that is? A person who doesn't even play that much to beat someone who plays every day? I think I've gotten better at the game, but I've also gotten smarter. Kofi always likes to play as the New England Patriots. We all know the New England Patriots are the best freakin' team in the whole game, so that's why he plays as them. So what do I do? I started playing as the New England Patriots so he couldn't. I make sure when we get to the team-select screen that I pick them first. As I got better at the game, I've switched over to the San Diego Chargers. Granted, the Browns are my favorite team, but I'm not playing as the Browns in *Madden*. You have to be some kind of video game guru to beat anybody as the Browns in *Madden*. So now I have my Chargers, and the last game me and Swoggle played, I beat him 28–14. He still owes me twenty dollars. Swoggle, if you're reading this, you still owe me twenty bucks.

The Abbot

Kofi Kingston

Miz and Hornswoggle both know that I am the *Madden* abbot and I run the *Madden* temple and give them lessons all the time. But as I can see, the lesson of humility has not been well taken by these two. To be honest, Hornswoggle lost to The Miz so bad that he really hasn't been the same since. He hasn't even played that much lately, the loss hit him that hard.

As far as The Miz, you know The Miz, he's a big talker, but last time we played I beat him 21–0. We have a 21-rule. It's the skunk rule, where if you're beating someone by 21, the game is over because you're basically just wasting your battery at that point. After Miz was doing all his talking about how he was going to pick the Patriots, he ended up switching up so he could pick whoever he perceives is the best team. If he manages to win one game with a team, whatever team that is, that's his new favorite team. No loyalty to the Browns . . . that's where he's from. But I'm from Boston, I'm a huge Patriots fan, so that's my team in the game, I play as the Pats. Last time we played, it was 21–0 and it wasn't even halfway through the first quarter. I don't think it was fun for him at all, but it was great for the rest of the car because it was one of the few times he actually shut up all tour.

Four

Lost

"We were seriously lost for my first ten years on the road."

—CHAVO GUERRERO

Rey Mysterio calls me from the road to break down his GPS obsession. "I love this thing," he says, and in the background I hear the GPS voice telling him to turn left. "I'm almost too obsessed with my navigation system, though, especially when I'm driving by myself. I'll go back in and punch in the address two or three times just to make sure I'm going to the right place." ☼ And why not, especially when one wrong turn can not only lead you in the wrong direction, it can sometimes even lead you to the wrong state.

Are There Mountains in Nebraska?

Chris Jericho

I can't believe we ever found our way anywhere before GPS. You'd drive into town completely blind and head to the gas station and ask where the arena is or where the wrestling is. Most big cities have signs on the road for the arenas, but other than that, you're really heading into these cities blind where you need to pull over and ask somebody where you're going. And the thing that's funny is, when you do this, you'll go to the gas station and you'll ask somebody where something is, and they'll say either, (a), it's two hours away, or, (b), it's five minutes away. And you can ask ten different people how far away something is and they'll give you ten completely different answers. Oh, it's about an hour away . . . Oh, it's about ten minutes away . . . Oh, it's about a half hour away. It's all people from the same town we're asking, and they're all giving us different answers. Where is it? People in general just have a really bad sense of direction, so I don't know how we got by without the GPS . . . or cell phones. I remember having to wait for a pay phone by the side of the road. Either that, or you'd wait by the phone in your hotel room for your girlfriend to call. You'd give her the room number and a time to call, and you would just sit and wait for that phone to ring. You would never go out because you were always waiting to talk to somebody. And it's hard to believe, that was only ten years ago. Now life on the road is a cakewalk compared to what it used to be like.

We used to get lost all the time, though. It was *Dumb and Dumber* out there on the road. I remember one time with Eddie Guerrero and Dean Malenko, we made a right turn instead of a left and we were supposed to be headed toward Nebraska, when all of a sudden we saw mountains. We ended up in like Oklahoma or Colorado and were all like, "Where the hell are we?" There was this other time when we had a show in Gainesville, Florida, and we ended up in Gainesville, Georgia. Just stupid crap like that would happen because nobody would ever bother checking anything.

But for the most part, Dean Malenko was the best road partner because he was like a human GPS. Sure, we might make the wrong turn before we got to the right city, but once we were there, he would remember everything about every town. "Take a right, then take a left down here, and after the alley you'll find the McDonald's." It didn't matter if we hadn't been in the town for two years, he just remembers everything. I always thought that it would've been smart to get an address book, and in this address book you put the town, say, Indianapolis. Then under the city name you put the gym you go to, the radio station you listen to, and the hotel you stay at. It would be so easy just to put all of this information together and just have it all in one place, because we go to the same towns over and over again, but you just forget after a while, and you're forced to find out all over again where you should stay and where you should work out. Every time you come back to the same town, you're forced to do the same work all over again. Stuff like that would make things a lot easier if I was a lot more organized, but I just wasn't. Now that there's GPS, you don't need to worry about it as much, but even the GPS will throw you off from time to time. Like today, I punched in a tanning place, and instead of calling the number, I just end up driving there, and fifteen minutes later I pull up to a place that doesn't even exist anymore. If only I was smarter, I would've had all that information in my address book.

The Two-Hour Turn

Rey Mysterio

One time I was on the road with Eddie Guerrero, and this was back before GPS, back before you could just punch in the address to your navigation, and I remember we were on the way to a show somewhere around Lubbock, Texas. We got turned around somehow and ended up driving two and a half hours in the wrong direction before we realized we were going the wrong way. When we realized it, we had to turn around and drive as fast as we could in order to still get to the show on time.

Usually when you're driving, you see the signs: thirty miles to wherever you're going, then twenty-five miles. But it was just one of those nights where we started talking about something, and the conversation was so good, neither one of us realized we were headed completely in the wrong direction. We just kept driving and talking, talking and driving, and then finally I asked him if he saw a sign to the city. He said no, so we decided to pull over and ask someone. Back then, that was our method of getting directions. So we stopped at a gas station, and they were like, "You guys are about two hundred miles away." Oh my

God, I couldn't believe it. It was already six o'clock and the show started at eight. We hustled as fast as we could and ended up making it to the show at about eight thirty. We were late, but we were still able to wrestle that night. We didn't miss the show, even with our bad sense of direction.

The Hangover

William Regal

I live a pretty boring life nowadays, but I didn't used to. I remember one time when myself, Ric Flair, Arn Anderson, and Bobby Eaton were on a loop from Arizona to Lancaster, California, so we decided to base ourselves in Las Vegas for what turned into a three-day bender. We were pretty wild back then, and basically, while we were in Las Vegas, I hadn't been to bed for three days. But on Monday, we needed to be in Lancaster, and it was Arn Anderson's idea for us to rent a car and drive from Vegas rather than flying to Los Angeles and driving to Lancaster from there. But as we go to the rental car agency, there were hardly any cars to be had, so we ended up settling for the most ridiculously small car you've ever seen. Ric Flair was absolutely horrified by even the look of this tiny car, as he was used to riding everywhere in limousines. But here we

were, the four of us crammed into this small car, all of us hung over and in need of some food before we get out of Las Vegas.

So we pull over to a Subway to get a sandwich, and while we're in there, let me just say that for the two weeks leading up to this moment, Ric Flair had been—I won't say bragging, but let's just say he'd been *overemphasizing* to all the boys that he had just opened up a new gym in St. Martin in the Caribbean. So we're inside this Subway, and Flair had just walked out and gotten into the car because he had decided he was going to drive us to Lancaster. But while I'm waiting for my sandwich, I hear on the radio inside the store that a huge hurricane had just ripped through St. Martin and wiped out the whole island. So I get back into the car and sit in the back, and I waited until we were about five miles outside of Vegas until I decided to tell him. "I just heard on the radio how a big hurricane just blew through St. Martin and is blowing everything away." Ric looked up at me through the rearview mirror and just went, "Oh no, brother." The look on his face, I just started laughing.

Now some people, when they get nervous they smash things up, but to me, I get lost in these giggle fits where I just can't stop laughing. I actually end up making myself ill from laughing so much. So I started laughing so much that Bobby Eaton started laughing, and there are bits of Subway coming down my nose by this point, and Arn Anderson sees this, so he started laughing. Flair had just spent over one hundred thousand dollars on gym equipment, and it all just blew away.

So we're driving farther and farther into the desert, and every once in a while I just break out laughing again, and that gets everyone else laughing except for Flair. He's absolutely out of his mind now as he just can't find the funny side to this, but we were all hung over driving through the middle of the desert, just driving and driving, when he says to me, "Get the map out. Are you sure we're going the right way?" So I took the map out, and I just read the map the way I saw it. He asked me where we were, and I said, "We're in the Mo-Jo Desert." He was like, "You stupid bastard, it's the Mojave Desert."

He then proceeded to cut a promo on us while he's driving. He started saying how he's the Nature Boy and how he's used to riding in jets and limousines, but for some reason he was lost in the middle of the desert with three drunk lunatics and the Gila monsters. So we're laughing even harder now and steam is just coming out of his ears at this point. Bobby Eaton then points to me and he says, "Lord keeps lizards." Bobby always called me "Lord" because back then I went by the name Lord Steven Regal.

Anyway, Flair then sees an opening to get the topic of conversation onto something else and get everything back to normal, so he asks me what kind of lizards I keep. I tell him, "I have a few of this and a few of that." And then he asks me, "Are they still alive?" And Arn Anderson says, "No, he's got them nailed to a board in his house."

That was it. That just pushed Flair completely over the edge. From his investment getting blown away to all the giggling in the back to now Arn taking the first somewhat normal conversation we've had in an hour and snapping at him, Flair just couldn't take it anymore. He slams the brakes on the car in the middle of the desert, gets out, and starts running around the car, screaming. "Raaahh!" Flair just lost it.

Eventually we get him back in the car and calm him down, and we still have to drive like three hundred miles to get to the show, and the whole time, I just keep breaking down laughing.

Now, this whole time, Flair is wearing this all-white suit. So I tell him, "You know what, Ric, I've been to Lancaster before and it's a bit dusty. You're wearing this nice all-white suit, so you might want to stop somewhere before we get to the arena and change." But he says, "Oh no, brother, I'm the Nature Boy, I wear suits." So I tell him, "There's nowhere to shower, there's nowhere to get clean once we're there, and the way the wind is picking up, you're going to be a mess."

"No, brother, I'm the Nature Boy," he tells me. "I'm wearing the suit." So we eventually get there after what seemed like the never-ending drive as we eventually find the right way through the desert, and I ask him one last time, "Are you sure you don't want to get changed?" And one last time he tells me, "No, brother, I'm the Nature Boy. I wear suits." So he jumps out of the car, slams the door, and right as he slams the door, a great big dust cloud blows all over him, and literally he's covered from head to toe. His blond hair, his white suit, his eyes—he's covered in red clay. He turns and looks at me like it's my fault. Like I've done something to cause this dust cloud to attack him. He just looked at me like, "You dirty, rotten bastard."

Life Before GPS

Chavo Guerrero

When I first started wrestling, there were no cell phones, no computers, no GPS, there was no iPod . . . none of that. You know what we had? Maps. We were lost for ten years. We were seriously lost for my first ten years on the road. We would have to constantly stop and ask for directions. All you have to do now is punch in the address on the GPS, and it tells you, "Turn right here, turn left here."

It's funny, because now when we get to a town, we'll tell a lot of the young guys, "Hey, there's a gym over here," or how there's a good place to eat down this road. They always want to know how we know where everything is, but we had to, we had to know this stuff. Back when I first started, you couldn't just punch in IHOP into the GPS and find something to eat. There was none of that. Life on the road is definitely a lot easier now thanks to technology. It was a lot tougher back when I first started. We were on the road more, and if you had someone who wasn't good at reading maps, you were constantly getting bad directions. There was a lot less food out there back then too, and what you did find was never as healthy as you can find today. Now you can go to a convenience store and get a Muscle Milk. There was none of that stuff before. We used to live on Snickers bars. Now you have protein all packaged for you. I remember when protein bars first came out, they were a lifesaver because now you had something to eat.

And think about trying to do all of this without computers. Now you can just jump on the Internet and make your own hotel reservation with the click of a button. Back then, we just drove until we saw a hotel and hoped they had a vacancy. In fact, we slept in a car many a night because we couldn't find a hotel. It was a lot harder when I first started, and the generation before me had it even harder. Every generation, it gets a little easier . . . but it's still not *easy*.

Five

Hotel Hell

"When someone doesn't have a lock on their door and someone else has a bloodstain on their wall, it's not hard to put two and two together."

—DREW McINTYRE

What do you do when you check into a hotel at three in the morning and can't sleep? If you're R-Truth, that might mean writing rap lyrics. "Sometimes late at night, when it's quiet, that's when you get your best ideas," he tells me. For Ezekiel Jackson, that's the time he finally gets to catch up on the scores of his favorite sports teams. "When I get to my room, I'm not a big partyer. Just get me a room with a TV and a bed and I'm good," he says. "When it's two in the morning and you're in some random city, all you can really do is kick back and watch *SportsCenter*. Two in the morning is when I catch up on all of those highlights I missed when I was on the road."

And while every trip would be a whole lot smoother if all you had to do was get to your room, relax, write lyrics, and watch sports, unfortunately for the WWE Superstars, that's not always (and sometimes never) the case. From sleazy hotels to mystery stains in random rooms, sometimes just finding a clean, safe place to sleep is the hardest part of the job.

Or as Tommy Dreamer puts it, "Some of the hotels we've had to stay in are absolutely disgusting. You wouldn't believe we actually paid money to rent these rooms."

These stories detail what goes on in a WWE hotel when things get downright dirty (and a little bizarre).

The Dirty Divas

Maria

I thought life on the road would be a little more . . . clean. I think that's the best way to explain it. Some of those hotels we stay in have giant bugs! You wouldn't believe it. There was this one night where I found a huge spider in my bed. So I throw the blankets off me and jump out of bed, and this spider is seriously coming to attack

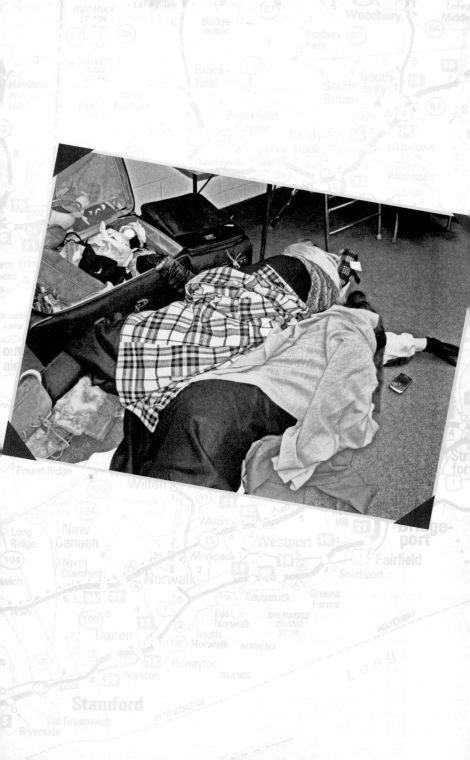

me as I'm getting out of bed. Five minutes later, I hear Layla start screaming, and there was a giant spider in her bed too. Then we look up on the wall and what do we see? Another spider! The next day, we got back to the room, and the spiders were gone, but there was this strange yellow beetle flying around. So I take a picture of it and Twitter it to show people what was in our room. Eve's brother sees this, and he tells us the official name, how it was an arachnid blah-blah-blah [not the official name], but it was hilarious. I guess I always thought life on the road would be more glamorous. But at the same time we have a lot more fun than I thought we would. We're all so close, and we all know even the smallest details about everyone. We know who sleeps well together—like I need to sleep by myself because otherwise I end up elbowing people in the face. But sometimes you have no choice and you have to share a bed because the hotels run out of rooms or they give you a room with only one bed. The other night this happened, and it was me, Layla, and Eve all in bed together. I hit Layla like three times with elbows while I was sleeping. I was trying to hug the side of the bed, but I guess I rolled over in the middle of the night and got her pretty good.

The other thing that happens in the hotel is we all tan each other. When we're getting ready for a show, it's like a fog of tanner overtakes the whole hotel. The Divas are actually the Dirty Divas, because we're pretty nasty.

In a pickle

Beth Phoenix

I traveled very little before I got on the road and started in the wrestling business, so it was all kind of new to me going from town to town to town. When I first started with WWE, the money wasn't really coming in yet, so I was trying to skimp and save every penny I could wherever I could. So I would go on Hotwire and look for the lowest stars of any hotel in town just so I could get the lowest prices.

I remember one time, it was only my second or third loop with *Raw*, and I ended up getting a place called something like the Econo Motel . . . something very generic like that, but when I pulled up, it looked more like the Bates Motel. It was one of those motels that was one floor, with the red roof where the doors accessed outside, and when I walk into the main area, all I see is this guy with two dirty socks up on the desk. He had a hole in one sock, he was smoking a cigar, and I see that his office looked more like an area where maybe he had been living. There were empty McDonald's wrappers everywhere, and the whole scene was just quite chaotic and filthy. All I wanted to do was get my key as fast as possible and lock the door to my room. I just remember, I'm walking to my room, and as I look around, there are shady characters everywhere. I hear yelling and screaming coming from different rooms, but I don't spook too easily. I just put my head down and went right to my room. But when I open the door and look inside, I notice this foul odor. I don't know what it is, but it's very pungent and smells like vinegar. I can't figure out what's going on in this room, so I turn around and flip on the lights, and at the foot of my bed is a smashed jar of pickles. No lie. I don't know why there are pickles in my room or how they got smashed, but that's the situation and the awful smell I am faced with.

But I was just so tired and it was the middle of the night, so I was just like, "Forget it." I'm not dealing with any of these people, I'm just going to change into my pajamas and go to bed. But when I head into the bathroom, I notice that inside is all just brick walls. The bathroom wasn't even finished being built. You could still see the mortar and everything. Then as I go to get into the bed, I flip open the comforter and there aren't even any sheets on the bed. I was like, "Econo Motel, you are gross." So what I did was I laid towels all over the comforters, then I slept with my jacket on and got out of there the first thing in the morning. And you know what? I can't stand the smell of pickles to this day. Of all the bizarre things to find in your room, I can't say that I would ever guess that one night I'd find a smashed jar of pickles. And I really don't want to know why or how they got there.

Disco Fever

Ted DiBiase

Randy Orton and I stayed at a Quality Inn near Penn State that seemed a bit sketchy. Not sketchy like we thought we were going to get robbed, but sketchy like there was a disco in the lobby with all these old people dancing at two in the morning when we checked in. Someone recognized us from the dance floor, and we both just put our heads down and ran to our rooms. It was the only hotel I've ever stayed at where I actually double locked the door and put the latch on. I feared for my life from these dancing old people. You see some strange things on the road, I'll tell you that, but you have to have a good time with it. You have to entertain yourself, and it's funny to sit back and think of things like that. I mean, what kind of hotel has a disco for old people in the lobby in the middle of the night?

Escape from L.A.

Mickie James

I use Hotwire a lot, but when I first started using it, I didn't understand how it worked. I was just looking for the best deal. So this one time, I was in Los Angeles and I booked a two-and-a-half-star hotel. Depending on where you are in the world, star ratings are different. So I'm thinking I'm going to get a Comfort Inn or something comparable. But I end up getting to this chain motel in L.A. that's out by the airport, and it was the scariest place I'd ever seen. The walls of my room were made of concrete, and literally, I heard gunshots all around. I seriously thought I was going to die that night. I was up all night. I couldn't sleep because the gunshots had me freaking out. That was the worst night I can remember.

But before I got to WWE, I'd travel wherever I could just so I could make it to the dance. I'd sleep in my car or find some cheap hotel for twenty dollars or whatever I could afford. But then once you're on the road full-time, you get accustomed to a certain level of comfort, or at least a soft bed. I couldn't even sleep in that bed in L.A. It was just too freaky. The room had two double beds, and when I heard the gunshots, I actually ducked down in between the two beds for extra protection. That was one night the clock just couldn't move fast enough for me.

Tyson Kidd

One night we show up to this hotel in Memphis, but there's nobody working the front desk, so this janitor or security-looking guy is the one who actually gives us our room key. But when we go up to the room, we realize that there's only one king-size bed for the three Hart Dynasty members. We go back downstairs to try and switch rooms, but there's nobody around. There's nobody working the front desk. Everyone is gone. So we can't change the room. Plus the air-conditioning in the hotel doesn't work, so not only are the Hart Dynasty going to get real close and all sleep in the same bed, we're going to sweat it out in this Memphis hotel in the middle of summer. It was bad. It's one thing to all share a bed, it's another thing to do it while we're all sweaty. And this has actually happened to us a few times, where we book two double beds, but when we show up the hotel is full and they can't switch us. That's when the Hart Dynasty bunks as one. It happens a lot more than it should.

The Rainbow Hotel

Tommy Dreamer

I was riding with Christian and Dolph Ziggler, and we had about a 290-mile drive in Canada. And there is nothing, and I mean nothing, along these highways along what is considered Midwest United States, but this is way up there in Canada. I think the drive was from Regina to Moose Jaw, or something ridiculous like that. There are no gas stations, there's nothing, so when you see a sign that this is your last place to fill up, you usually want to do it because you're not going to find anything else for at least a hundred or so miles. Anyway, it was getting close to the end of summer, and we didn't know that a lot of people vacation around the spot we were headed, and all of the hotels around the location were already booked up. So we drove about halfway, and there was not a hotel to be found with a vacancy. We looked everywhere until we finally stumbled across this one hotel called the Rainbow Hotel, and it was basically, what I feel, a hotel you rent by the hour, not the night . . .

it was not a nice hotel whatsoever. They also knew how much the hotels cost in the area and knew everything was booked, and they got us for like a hundred dollars for a prison-cell–type hotel room. A lot of times you're traveling, and you'll see your fellow WWE Superstars at the show, but you won't see them at the hotels. But I guess all of the people who were on that card realized that this was one of the only places with a vacancy, so here came Cryme Tyme, Mike Knox, Vladimir Kozlov, the Bella Twins, John Morrison, CM Punk, Melina . . . they probably had about fifteen WWE Superstars all staying at this one disgusting hotel.

My room, the guy didn't have a key to get me inside, so he had to actually come with me and open the door for me. So I asked him, "What if I have to leave?" And he said, "You can't. If you do, you're just going to have to leave your door open." So I didn't even have a key to my own room and I couldn't leave. You couldn't even close the bathroom door because whoever designed it put the door in last, and you would hit the toilet with the door, so it wouldn't even close. I mean, seriously, who designed this place? There were brown stains in the washtub and it was just a gross hotel. My bed was a single, and I slept with my clothes on because everything just looked so dirty. And worst of all, my room had these windows that were so low, any crook could've climbed inside my room in the middle of the night. All they had to do was push on the window, and they could've climbed right in.

So I ended up moving the refrigerator against the door just to make sure nobody could get in. I figured if I didn't have the key, I didn't know who did. Then I put my suitcase up against the window so at least if anyone tried to get in I could hear it. Things were really that bad. I mean, this was seriously the worst hotel I've ever been to. We got in around three in the morning, hoping we could at least get some sleep, and when I'm investigating my room, Christian shoots me a text saying that his room was so bad, so disgusting, that he couldn't take it any longer and decided to sleep in the car.

The next morning, we're all swapping stories of how bad our rooms were, and as we pull out of the parking lot, we see that behind the hotel is a cemetery. Just when we thought our hotel couldn't get any worse, we see the cemetery.

Rainbow Hotel, part 2

Drew McIntyre

Oh yeah, the Rainbow Hotel. First hotel I've ever stayed at where there were bloodstains on the wall and

dead roaches in the shower. It's one of the only places where you had a group of these big, tough wrestlers worried about their safety. When someone doesn't have a lock on their door and someone else has a bloodstain on their wall, it's not hard to put two and two together. The funniest thing about staying there, though, was showing up at the arena the next day. Morrison walks up and says, "I stayed at the worst hotel ever last night." And then Christian would be like, "No, my hotel was the worst." Then CM Punk said, "Nothing can top the disgusting place I stayed." No one realized until the next day that we were all staying at the same place. Ask anyone who was there, and they'll tell you, this was the single worst hotel they have ever stayed at. When you have guys blocking their doors and sleeping out in their cars, you know things are beyond bad.

Then to make matters worse, that same trip, after we left the Rainbow Hotel, I was traveling with the Bella Twins and the trunk on our rental car broke. So we had to go buy some bungee cords at the Home Depot just to keep the trunk closed. Luckily for us, nothing was stolen. I'm surprised, too, because it was open all night while we were inside the Rainbow Hotel. Maybe the cemetery spooked all the thieves.

The Overflow

Evan Bourne

Since I was eighteen years old, I've never really stayed in the same place. Until I got to WWE developmental, I was never even in the same city for more than a week. I'd be sleeping in four or five beds a week. It's just standard for us. So life on the road, that's just what it is . . . lots of different beds and the ability to live out of three different bags and a rental car for the rest of your life.

Typically wrestlers, what we do now is use Hotwire. It has great rates, and it lets you know the amenities of each hotel. Two stars is really cheap, two and a half stars is pretty cheap, three stars is a pretty decent rate, and four is your high-end rate that is usually over one hundred dollars. Usually we stay at the three-star hotels, but every once in a while you make a concession to go down to a two-star just because it's available, it's cheap, and it's right by the airport. Besides, most of the time, we're only in our rooms to sleep, so how bad could it be?

Well, let me tell you about my two-and-a-half-star hotel in New Jersey. It was right by the airport, and I thought it would be great. But then I get dropped off at the front office and say, "Hi, I made a reservation under Hot-wire." I give him my name, and the guy looks at me and shakes his head. That's all he would do, shake his head. I was like, "What does that mean?" And he finally says, "We don't have any rooms."

"But I already paid for this room," I tell him. "You have to have a room because I paid for it. That's the whole point of making the reservation and paying in advance." Next thing I know, the guy is making me fill out some paper-work, all the usual—name, address, phone number—and he's like, "Yeah, room 32, right up there."

I lug my bags up the stairs, and the room looks pretty decent, until I go into the bathroom. When I flushed the toilet, everything backed up to the point water started pouring over the side of the toilet and flooding the bath-room. Water hit the side of the tub, then it hit the other wall, and the water just kept on coming. I couldn't believe how much water was flooding my room after just one flush. It was literally a disaster. And this was at like one, one thirty in the morning. So I knew I wanted out. I looked out my hotel-room window, looked up the street, looked down the street, and saw a sign for Dunkin' Donuts in the distance. I made sure I had my wallet and my cell phone, and I went for a walk. Twenty minutes later I get to the old Dunkin' Donuts and hang out there for an hour. Got a donut, a coffee, and a cheese-whatever, then I got some more, then I started my long walk back to the hotel. When I was on my way back, I stumbled upon a gentlemen's club that was halfway between the Dunkin' Donuts and my hotel. And that's where I spent the rest of my night. The club was alcohol free, so I just sat there and drank bottled water and enjoyed myself.

Blame It on Eve

Tyson Kidd

One weird trip was this time we were headed to New York City for TV. In our car was the Hart Dynasty and the Great Khali. And then, whoever Eve was riding with originally on the loop had to go to *Raw*, so now Eve was riding with us to New York as well. We're all crammed in this car. And Khali, he has to sit like this—it's not his fault, but he has to sit in the front seat with the seat leaning all the way back. So whoever is sitting behind him, and it's usually me, Khali is right in your lap. We always try to make things easier for Khali, and I have a hotel room where Khali is staying, but we decide we're going to drop off Khali, then drive Eve to her hotel, which is totally out of the way, then we're going to drive back to our hotel. So we drop Khali off, and this is after a show and after eating, so this is like three in the morning, and now we're driving Eve back to her hotel, but there is all this construction on the road, so now it's like four in the morning. On our GPS, it says we're going to get back to our hotel at five, and there's all the same construction we just drove through in order to get back. So we decide to forget it, we're just going to look up hotels and stay at the closest one to us. We end up finding some little rat-hole hotel in New York, but we figure it's worth it just to save the time. But when we get to the hotel, the room is so hot, we can't even breathe. To make things worse, the people staying in the room above us were running around, and the walls and floor were so thin, it sounded like these people were in our room. I didn't sleep the whole night at all. Then the next morning, we had to go back and drive another hour to go pick up Khali and take him to the building. And guess what? The hotel we were originally going to stay at was right next to the arena. The moral of the story: Don't help Eve. And that's because she's associated with Cryme Tyme. Don't ever help out anyone associated with Cryme Tyme. That's my recommendation.

Roll of the Dice

Chris Jericho

If you go to one hotel and it's sold out, that usually means that all of the hotels in that area are going to be sold out, and that means you have problems. There have been plenty of times when Eddie Guerrero and myself and this referee named Mark Curtis had to sleep in the car in the parking garage of the airport. I'd put my alarm on the dash so we didn't sleep late, then I'd brush my teeth with a bottle of water and go from there. There are other times when you wish you slept in your car because you get to your room, there are towels everywhere, pubic hairs on the toilet, stains on the carpet that you don't even want to know where they came from. You never really know what you're going to get, especially if you're not smart enough to make your own reservations. Sometimes you just roll the dice and hope for the best with the type of room you're going to get.

Not the Best Time for a Swim

Nikki Bella

We are in Green Bay, and we are staying in this hotel that also has a casino. So after dinner and a few glasses of wine, I tell Brie, "C'mon, let's just go to bed. We have to catch our flights in the morning." But she was like, "No, no, let's go to the casino." But I kept telling her, "No, it's time to go to bed." So we get to our room and I'm getting into bed, but she is stomping up and down on the bathroom floor. I can hear her in there because the floor was this loud tile. She was stomping, trying to wake me up, like, "I want to go to the casino." So I tell her, "Brianna, are you serious right now? Just go to bed." So she gets into bed, and I fall asleep. Next thing I know I'm woken up by someone knocking on the door. I look over, and there's no Brie. So I hurry up and answer the door, and there's Brie. She's standing there dripping wet in her white dress, with two security guards on each arm. Security was like, "Excuse me, miss, is this your sister? We found her at the pool swimming laps by herself." I was like, "Brie, get in this room right now!" It was like three in the morning, and she was down there swimming laps in an all-white dress that went above her knees. I couldn't believe it.

Blame It on the a-a-Alcohol

Brie Bella

If there's a pool, you'll find Brie in there, it doesn't matter the hour of the night or what clothes I have on. That's just the way I am . . . especially if I've had a few drinks first. And that's basically what happened that night in Green Bay. I just wanted to go to the casino so bad, but my sister wouldn't go with me, and you know how when you're a little intoxicated, things get exaggerated in your mind. So I was mad she wouldn't come to the casino. I was just like, "Screw this, I'm going for a swim." It wasn't the smartest thing I ever did because I totally ruined my white dress, but at least I remembered to take my shoes off so I didn't ruin those as well. If you want to know anything else about this story, you'll have to ask Jose Cuervo.

Brood Awakening

Tommy Dreamer

Whenever I travel with Edge and we only have a few hours of sleep until we need to catch our early-morning flight, we'll end up sharing a room just to save money. I will always want to go to bed, but a lot of times Edge will be so amped up, he'll want to go out and stay up all night before our flight. Then, of course, he'll call in his partner in crime, Christian, and I'll be dozing off and then all of a sudden someone will do a Superfly Splash off their bed onto me or someone will drop an elbow on me while I'm sleeping, and then we basically have some sort of semifight because they're both pulling covers off of me or wrapping the covers around me while they double-team me just to wake me up. So what always happens is, they get me woken up, I'm all wound up and fired up, and then they wind up going to bed.

The new gambit

Kofi Kingston

When things really get crazy is late at night in the hotel. When Hornswoggle and I check in, we both get a copy of the key. Then as soon as we get in the door, we know it's time to be on alert because we try to throw the keys at each other like Gambit from X-Men. And those things hurt if they get you in the right spot.

At first we never hit each other, then one time he hit me in the eye, so I tried to lock myself in my room. But then when I tried to get out, I realized that there was this hair dryer that was attached to the wall, and the cord was just long enough that Hornswoggle wrapped it around the door handle. So he locked me in my room. We got a good kick out of that, but there's always shenanigans going on inside the hotel.

Hornswoggle

Oh yeah, the ninja hotel keys. It all started when he and I started sharing rooms to save money. I like two-star hotels. I like to save money. Kofi stays in nothing but three-star and above, but it's really just a waste of money. But anyway, ninja hotel keys all started one night when he walked in the room, I picked up a key and I whipped it at him, and it hit him in the face. That's when the war started. I'm still winning the war, as he has a lot of catching up to do. He finally caught me in the cheek the other day, and it was great. I actually applauded him. But then I also tied the door to his suite shut with a blow dryer to get back at him. He then proceeded to rip the blow dryer off the wall, and it cost me $150. He still owes me the money to this day.

six

Good (and Bad) Eats

"When you're on the road, it's not just about finding

something to eat . . . it's about making sure it doesn't come

back to get you."

—CHAVO GUERRERO

Finding something to eat at four in the morning can be a

challenge. Scratch that—finding something *healthy* to eat at

four in the morning is the real challenge. "I'm a big fan of the

Wendy's Baconator," Kane confesses with a laugh. Make

that a Double and we're talking almost 1,000 calories and

2,260 mg of sodium in one meal . . . and that doesn't even count

fries and a drink. Yikes. "That's one of the worst parts about

life on the road, all the fast food you end up eating as you

travel from one stop to the next," he says. Then again, when

you're a WWE wrestler, sometimes finding a place to sit down and eat healthy is only half the battle. The other half? Eating with each other.

One Man's Trash . . .

The Miz

I used to travel with Elijah Burke, and let me tell you, Elijah Burke is a character. Whenever we were on the road, we would stop at Cracker Barrel or Denny's or a Waffle House, whatever we could find open late at night. And every time Elijah would sit down, he would immediately ask the waitress for a glass of hot water. She would bring the hot water, and he would stick all of his silverware into the hot water. I'd ask him why, and he'd say, "Daddy, have you seen the silverware here? There are spots everywhere on it." Okay, I'll let that go. But then we would get our food, and I would have some extra fries left. Now, if you're a nice guy at the table and you have extra fries, you always ask the other person at your table, "Do you want my fries?" That's the nice thing to do. So here I am, "Elijah, would you like my fries?" And he's like, "How dare you, Daddy!" He's screaming at me in the middle of a restaurant, and all of these old people inside Cracker Barrel start turning around wondering what's happening. "How dare you offer

me trash! That is your trash!" Elijah is screaming at me. "That is your trash, Daddy!"

I'm like, "Elijah, this isn't my trash. I'm done eating it." And he says, "You're done eating it? Well, where does it go when you're done eating it?" So I tell him, "Well, when the waitress takes it, she puts it in the trash."

"That's right," he says. "She puts it in the trash."

So we actually went around and started an argument through the entire restaurant whether extra fries on a plate are trash. We're asking all of these old women, like, "Ma'am, excuse me, but if I had extra fries and I was offering them to you, would that be me offering you trash?" And this one little old lady tells us, "No, I don't think so." And Elijah yells out, "Are you kidding! That is trash. You're telling me you would eat this man's trash?" This poor lady is like, "Well, I wouldn't eat his fries because I don't really know him, but I would eat my husband's fries."

Elijah just looks at her and says, "I can't believe you eat trash. That is disgusting."

Needless to say, I can't believe this guy. He's incredible. But that's not where the weird late-night food stories end with Elijah Burke. This other night we go to Denny's, and let me tell you, Elijah loves carrot cake. "Love" might not even be a strong enough word for how Elijah feels about carrot cake. Anyway, the waitress comes over after our meal and asks us if we'd like dessert. "I'd love dessert. In fact, I'd love carrot cake. Thank you very much," he says. Then she asks me if I want dessert, but I tell her I'm full and that I don't want anything. Elijah can't believe I didn't want anything. "Daddy, she's giving us free carrot cake."

"Elijah, she's not giving us free carrot cake."

"But she offered it to us," he says.

So I tell him, "It's her job to ask us if we want dessert. She's just doing her job."

"Now, now, now, now, now, Daddy, she's giving it to us for free. Trust me on this. You should get a piece of carrot cake from her and give it to me. Get it to go so I can take it with me on the airplane."

"Elijah," I tell him, "she's not giving this to us for free." But he just keeps insisting until I finally give in and ask for a piece of carrot cake. Lo and behold, what's on the receipt? Carrot cake.

"But you offered it to me, ma'am," Elijah insists. The poor waitress tries to explain that after every meal, they ask if you'd like dessert, but he sits there and complains for a half an hour. Half an hour about stupid carrot cake. Half an hour over $4.95. That is what he is complaining about. I paid for my carrot cake just to give it to him, but he didn't pay for his carrot cake. She gave it to him for free. She actually took it out of her check, just for Elijah Burke.

No Shakes for You

John Morrison

My biggest pet peeve is any time we go anywhere and it's late, the first thing that all of the fast food places do is turn their shake machines off. And it's only because they're lazy. I don't know what it is—that they don't want to make the shakes or they don't want to clean their machines. But it doesn't matter where you go, whether it's McDonald's or Wendy's or wherever, my favorite cheap meal is a milk shake, and whenever we pull in, I just have this sixth sense of when the shake machine is going to be turned off.

No Translation Necessary

D'Lo Brown

This is back in 1998, when Taka first came to the company. He didn't speak any English, and he was the only Japanese guy there at the time. So Jim Ross sees me as the responsible one and he tells me, "Hey, we've got this kid

Taka here, he doesn't speak any English. For a couple of road trips, can you take him on the road with you? Since he can't speak English, he can't read road signs, so we don't want him to drive." So Taka, the whole time, all he would say to me was, "Thank you, D'Losan . . . okay, okay." That's all the English he knew.

So we were doing a show in West Virginia one night and we flew into Columbus. It's about a four-hour drive to Huntington, and after the show, we're driving back to Columbus in the middle of the night. The highway we're riding on is this desolate, two-lane highway, and about halfway through, we see this oasis of two gas stations, a McDonald's, and a Burger King. In the car it was me, The Rock, Mark Henry, Grandmaster Sexay, and Taka, and Taka was sleeping in the back. I'm driving along and I'm like, "Guys, what do you want to eat?" Everyone chimes in, but Taka's still sleeping. Mind you, it's about two o'clock in the morning at this point, so I start yelling, "Taka, what do you want to eat?" Taka shakes his head, looks up, and says, "McDonald's or Burger King, it doesn't really matter to me." Taka then closes his eyes like he's about to go back to sleep, then he realizes that he just spoke in perfect English. He sits up and says, "Ah, D'Losan, McDonald's or Burger King . . . okay, okay." He knew how to speak English the whole time but he was just pretending not to know English. He even tried to go back to his Pidgin English, but I told him, "You let the genie out of the bottle now." All he could say was, "Oh, I'm sorry. My boss told me to keep it a secret that I know English." We all got on him after that and gave him the keys. Here we were chauffeuring him, now it was his turn to drive. All this time, we've been trying to help him around, and you've got Rocky talking to him like he's a five-year-old kid, and the whole time, the guy speaks better English than Mark Henry.

Nose Plugs, please

Maria

Natalya and Eve love to eat corn nuts, and I hate the smell of them. I'll be sitting in the car trying to plug my nose. The smell of corn nuts is gross. I remember one night in Tampa, I was traveling with Layla and there was nothing open, so we stop at a gas station, and as they're stocking up on corn nuts, I buy three packs of tuna and a bottle of mayonnaise. This store had a hot dog stand, so I took some relish and onions and I stirred it into my tuna in this big to-go cup, and I ended up eating it with crackers. It didn't make me sick or anything, but it sure did smell bad in the car. Not corn nut bad, but it was bad.

The Shakes

Chavo Guerrero

Late-night food is awful. The Waffle House is open 24/7, so a lot of times that's all you can eat. I've done it before where I had Waffle House at three in the morning and I ate a chicken breast that wasn't totally cooked, so I had them cook it more. The very next day I was sick to my stomach. I remember I was in Florida at the time, and the sickness started to really kick in. I couldn't even wrestle that day it got so bad. I was just sitting there shaking. Billy Kidman actually had to drive me to a hotel by the airport, and I couldn't even get out of the car without help. I was sitting in my room, and my back just started really tightening up. I don't know if it was because of cramps or what, but my back was really tight. I was freezing cold, I'm throwing up, and now even though I'm freezing, I had to put ice on my back because it was so tight I couldn't even lie down. It was a horrible night, and that's happened to me a few times. When you're on the road, it's not just about finding something to eat . . . it's about making sure it doesn't come back to get you.

And when it comes to eating, we got bad habits all

over the place. We all come from different walks of life, so what works in one place might not work in another. We have people who like to eat with their mouths open and smacking their food. We have people farting all over the place. A guy like Big Show will stink out the bus until finally we're all yelling at him to stop farting or we'll all kick his butt. That's what it takes, because not one of us could kick his butt by ourselves, but if there are ten of us, we could do it.

Miller Time

IRS

One night we had a show at the Boston Garden, and during the show, the Iron Sheik had asked me if he could catch a ride with me back to Hartford so he could make it to the airport. But he was in a match that was on a little bit later than mine, so I told him I'd give him a ride, but we needed to leave before the show was over. So he has his match, then he just grabs his bag and walks out with me still in his wrestling gear, with his curled-up boots. It's a Sunday in Boston, and you can't buy beer on Sunday in Massachusetts, but Sheik says, "No, no, Mike Baba, I know this guy across the street from the Boston Garden." So we pull up to what looks like a bar—it had these big bay windows that you could see through—and Sheik goes in the bar and I see his hands moving and they're talking back and forth as Sheik tries to convince the guy to sell him some beer.

This went on for like fifteen minutes before Sheik finally convinced the guy to sell him some beer. But sure enough, this took so long that here comes everyone out of the Boston Garden, and as people leave the building, they all see Sheik inside the bar in his wrestling gear. So they all start banging on the windows and they're yelling, "That's the Iron Sheik." Meanwhile, I'm still in the car and I'm trying to scoot down as far as I can in my seat so no one will recognize me. Then finally, the Sheik comes out and gets into the car with a bag of beer, but now the fans all turn their attention to our car. They're pounding our windows and shaking our car from side to side. I thought, "Well, this is the end of my life." We had a pretty good mob surrounding our car to the point where we couldn't even drive along the street. I actually had to jump the car onto the sidewalk just to maneuver around to a spot where we could get back on the road where traffic was moving and get on the highway. Both of us, our hearts were racing. It's pretty scary when you have that many people out there shaking your car and pounding on your windows. Finally, we're on the highway, and Sheik opens up a beer and says, "Oh well, at least the beer tastes good."

Instant Karma

Kofi Kingston

One night I was traveling with Cryme Tyme, and we were driving to D.C., and we stopped at a Roy Rogers because it was open twenty-four hours. I get in line, JTG gets in line, and we're trying to meander our way around. Then Shad cuts in front of us . . . but this is karma at its best. Shad is looking at the food, and they didn't have any chicken. So here is big Shad, a 6'8", 285-pound guy, and he asks this lady if they have any chicken, and she totally punks him out. She was like, "Does it look like we have chicken? Don't you think if we had chicken it would be out there with all of the rest of the food?" It was just hilarious to see Shad get punked out by some lady with a hairnet. Shad just couldn't say anything. He was speechless. But that was karma. Had he not cut us in line, then it would've been one of us asking about the chicken and getting yelled at by the hairnet lady.

Dolph Ziggler

My one guilty pleasure on the road is eating almonds. Almonds are pretty healthy for you, so I justify it by getting the chocolate-covered almonds and going low carb all day, then every once in a while waking up with an empty bag next to me.

I Don't Like Mustard

Matt Hardy

Life on the road is definitely challenging. First and foremost, when you've been doing this for a while and you start to get your body beat up, it turns into a full-time job just keeping your body together. Here, your body is your business. Your body is your product. People always ask me when I go to the gym. My response is, "Whenever I can." If you work for WWE, even the people who look like they don't go to the gym, they go to the gym. If you wrestle on a full-time basis, you go to the gym. You just have to. If you don't, your ligaments and tendons are just going to fall apart. It takes a very special animal to do what we do.

That being said, you won't survive in this business for any amount of years unless you truly have the passion of loving the sport, and I do, and I know Jeff does as well. You have to look at what we do and see what it does to your body, and you have to realize that later in life, this is going to influence my health. This is going to affect my health. And I truly accept this. My motto is this: You only live one time, and I would rather have some aches and pains while living an amazing seventy-five years, than living a dull eighty-five years.

I'm thirty-four right now, and I promise you, I've lived a life gazillions of people wish they lived. I couldn't begin to tell you how great my life has been. Not only living my dream day after day, but this has also been very financially rewarding. And beyond even that, it's just nice to wake up every morning and know that I'm doing what I love.

To think that any week, I could be getting off a plane and be in any country in the world, that's still amazing to me. It's mind-blowing to me. And part of the reason why it's so amazing goes hand in hand with another one of my mottoes: It's not necessarily where you're at, it's who you're with. If I'm with my brother or if I'm with some good friends, then we'll make a good time out of a

370-mile drive. We'll plug in the iPod, we'll have some Kings of Leon playing, we'll stop to eat a couple of times, tell some stories, joke around, and have a good time.

I'm trying to retrain myself, though, because I'm in a real bad habit of going to bed at four or five in the morning and waking up around eleven. That's just how my schedule is now. Even when I'm home, I have about four other business projects I'm working on. So during the day, I'm training or doing work. But when it gets to be around one in the morning, that's what I love because that's my alone time. My favorite thing to do at home is to sit back around two or three in the morning in my hot tub, maybe have a cocktail like a vodka cranberry, and just relax. I live on 140 acres, and there are no neighbors nearby. That's when I can see a sky full of stars and just relax. To me, that's the ultimate form of relaxation. And when I'm having a tough time on the road, all I have to do is think ahead to the next time I'll be home sitting back in the hot tub, looking at those stars.

But that's not the only thing I miss about home. There is this place about ten minutes away from my house called the Checkered Flag. It's a truck stop that stays open twenty-four hours. It's a real hole in the wall, mom-and-pop–type joint, but they have the most amazing hamburgers, cheeseburgers, and hot dogs you can ever eat. There will be nights when we're all hanging out at like four in the morning, and we'll call our buddy to come pick us up and take us to the truck stop. I'll get my cheeseburger with no mustard. I don't like mustard. That was a Matt Fact that people liked a lot, that I dislike mustard—but anyway, I get mine without mustard and Jeff gets his all the way, and we sit back in this truck stop and we'll eat cheeseburgers and fries. That's truly our guilty pleasure. We talk about it all the time when we're on the road. We'll be sitting in a hotel in Texas or California or wherever, and one of us will say, "Man, nothing would beat a truck stop cheeseburger right about now."

Seven

The Swerve

"I walked out of the hotel and was like, 'Why is V sitting on that guy?' "

—KANE

An unexpected plot twist. A story you think is heading in one direction that suddenly shifts and takes you to a whole other, shocking place. That's what you call a "swerve." Throughout my months collecting stories for this book, there were a few times when I couldn't even believe what I was hearing. "Did this really happen?" I would ask, and every time, the Superstar would just stop and laugh. "Just like I said," they would repeat, "just like I said." ☼ What can I say? When you travel more than two hundred days a year, something insane is bound to happen.

Beating a Dead Horse

Shelton Benjamin

One night, I almost beat up Brian Kendrick over the movie *Seabiscuit*. We were in Canada, and we had the day off. There were a whole bunch of us there, including my partner at the time, Charlie Haas, and the referee Mike Chioda, and we all decided we were going to go out and get something to eat. We were all staying at this resort, and basically the town we were in was built around this resort. So we decided we were going to walk through the town to find a nice restaurant. But before I could even leave, the whole group left me for some reason and headed off to the restaurant without me. I'm walking around and I'm trying to find where they went, but no one would call me back or answer their phones. Luckily, I just happen to stumble into the right restaurant, but by the time I get in there, everyone had already ordered and was eating their food, so I sit down and basically start acting like a brat. I'm like, "Why did you guys leave me? Some friends you are." It was all in fun, though, I was just busting everyone's chops. At some point, the topic of conversation switched over to movies, and *Seabiscuit* was out in theaters at the time. But as soon as someone brought up *Seabiscuit*, Brian Kendrick started yelling, "Nobody talk about *Seabiscuit*. Nobody talk about *Seabiscuit*. I haven't seen it yet and I want to see it."

Mind you, I have still never seen that movie, but I blurt out, "You want to know what happened, I'll tell you what happened. The horse lost the race and died because his friends left him at the gate." I'm basically playing off the fact that they all left me, but Kendrick starts going crazy. I don't know what he was thinking, or what he thought he heard, but he looks at me and says, "I told you not to ruin it for me."

I had just made a salad, and as soon as he said that, he pours a whole glass of water in my salad. I looked at him and was like, "What the hell are you doing?"

And he told me, "I told you not to ruin the movie for me!"

"Are you kidding me?" I said. "I haven't even seen that movie. Didn't you hear me? I was joking about how you guys left me."

He started stuttering, like, "Oh, oh . . ." And I'm like, "You owe me a new salad. You ruined my salad. Now you need to go make me a new one."

He just looked at me with this bewildered look, then he said, "Dude, I'm not making you another salad."

I couldn't believe it. First they left me, then I make a

joke about a movie I've never seen, and now this guy who just dumped a glass of water in my salad won't make me a new salad. To make matters worse, he started back with the whole "I can't believe you ruined the movie for me."

We were like two kids, and up until this point I was laughing pretty hard. But then he completely changed his tone. He looked at me one more time and said, "I'm not making you another salad." And as soon as his tone changed and it wasn't funny anymore, my tone changed and I told him, "You're going to make me another salad or I'm going to whoop you."

So he told me, "Go ahead and whoop me. I get my butt kicked for a living."

Only thing is, this time, it was going to be real.

Now, all of a sudden, the whole mood of the table changed and everyone is tense. Charlie was like, "I'll make you a salad, don't worry about it." And Charlie actually got up and made me a salad and brought it to me, but I was like, "No! He ruined it, so he's going to make me another one."

Finally, after about five really tense minutes, I told him, "As soon as we walk out that door, I'm going to whoop your ass. Bottom line."

So now we're sitting there and I'm staring a hole through him and I have every intention of beating him up.

Finally he gets up, throws together a little lettuce in what can only be described as an insult of a salad, and tosses it in front of me. Leaves were flying everywhere, and he says, "There you go, tough guy."

As soon as the plate landed in front of me, I picked it up and threw it at him. I told him, "Who do you think you're messing with? You ever try something like that again, and I'm going to kick your ass."

Everyone was quiet, and Nidia grabbed me and brought me outside to cool things off. I don't even remember if I finished my dinner or not, I was still so mad at that point, but we made it out of the restaurant without incident.

Now, mind you, I'm still feeling like beating him up, and I don't know what he's thinking, but the very next day, we get to work, and guess who's wrestling each other. It was one of those things where I could've made things worse, because when I showed up to work, I still wanted to beat him up, but I had to do the professional thing and put my personal feeling aside for the sake of the show. It was in the back of my mind to whip his ass the whole match, but he later apologized and everything, and we always tell this story and we still laugh about it today.

Of all the movies for two wrestlers to fight over, would you have ever guessed it would be *Seabiscuit?*

Roman Candles

Goldust

I remember Owen Hart used to always drive with one of his friends when he was in town. And this one night we were driving from Youngstown, Ohio, to Pittsburgh, and I see Owen and his friend are behind us on the road. I'm driving with Billy Gunn, Davey Boy Smith, and Bob Holly, and we were all the fun, rowdy type, and I remember we all pulled over to go to the bathroom. When Owen and his friend got out of their shiny white car, Davey Boy lit three smoke bombs and threw them in Owen's friend's car when they were busy peeing. As we got in our car to leave, I look in the rearview mirror and all you see is this green and yellow smoke coming out of the car. Smoke is everywhere, Owen is laughing his ass off, and his friend is freaking out because he thinks his car is on fire.

We pull up a little bit, then we slow down and let them catch up, and Davey Boy leans out the window with these Roman candles and starts shooting them at this guy's car. They're bouncing off the windshield, and this guy starts speeding up. I don't know how pissed off he is, but I know Owen is in the car, and Owen was always the instigator, so I'm sure he was in there just driving the guy crazy. Meanwhile, we're flying down the freeway at around eighty miles per hour still shooting these Roman candles at his hood, and we're throwing firecrackers out the windows at them any time they got close.

I remember the next day, looking at this guy's car, and it was black. This used to be a white car, but now it was a freakin' mess with black smoke marks all over it. There were burn holes in the carpet from the smoke bombs . . . but he didn't care. He was just a big fan of Owen's, they were friends, so he was like, "It's cool." I'll never forget that. It wasn't even a rental. It was his car. Actually, it was a white van, or at least it used to be white.

One of the funniest things about that night is when we were driving out on the turnpike, we were way ahead of them and they were trying to catch up, but I was hauling ass at this point, so they weren't even close. I decided to pull over into a ditch and turn off the headlights so they wouldn't see us. I wanted to let them pass us so I could fly up behind them with our lights off, get up on their ass, and shoot at them some more. So we do that, we're all sitting there in the dark, and we see them haul ass trying to find us. I pull out of the ditch real slow, the lights are off, and all you see is black. They're hauling ass over this hill, but they couldn't really see behind them, and they couldn't find us.

So I pull right up on their ass, and I'm talking about within a foot of their car, and I'm just hoping they don't slam on the brakes. So here goes Davey Boy, he lights up another Roman candle and—*voom!*—he starts shooting it at their back window. I turned on the brights and started honking the horn trying to freak them out. It was crazy . . . and a little dangerous.

Press Slammed

Kane

When you walk out of your hotel and see Big Daddy V sitting on someone, you know something crazy just went down. And that's exactly what happened one time in England. We were all getting off the bus in either Manchester or Birmingham in the UK. Anyway, we were pulling into the hotel, it was really late, and there had been a kickboxing match at the arena across the street and all of the fans were headed toward our hotel. Next thing we know, one of their fans punched one of our security guards and there was a short scuffle. Our guys were all very professional actually, but what stopped the whole fight was Big Daddy V sitting on two people. That was the end of the fight. I walked out of the hotel and was like, "Why is V sitting on that guy?"

The next day, I read about it in the English papers, and the British newspapers are even worse than our press when it comes to sensationalizing things, and the paper had an interview with the kickboxing promoter. So of course, he told this self-serving story of how there was this huge fight between all of his guys and all of our guys, and he's talking about how we're tossing people around with suplexes and all his guys are throwing big roundhouse kicks at us . . . and none of it happened. Don't believe everything you read in the press.

Wee-Man

Kofi Kingston

Ever since the draft, I've been traveling with Hornswoggle. We were in New Orleans one time, and I actually got to the hotel first, but the garage was full so I had to park along the street. The next morning, I was walking with Hornswoggle out to the car, and when I go to put the bags in the trunk, I notice this guy with dreadlocks and gold teeth riding an old-school BMX bike. I look at him, and I see he's staring at us, then all of a sudden he slams on the brakes. He's looking at Hornswoggle, and we know he's going to say something, then he starts yelling, "Hey, shorty, hey, shorty, I see you." Then he called Hornswoggle Wee-Man. He thought Hornswoggle was Wee-Man from *Jackass.*

What's funny is, we always call Hornswoggle Wee-Man because everyone always mistakes the two of them. Hornswoggle hates being called that. And now here is this guy with gold teeth riding a bike calling him Wee-Man first thing in the morning.

Then later that night, we went down to Café du Monde, which is this old French place in New Orleans, and one of the waiters was so sure he knew who we were. He wanted our autographs and everything, but he had no idea. He thought we were all the *Jackass* guys, and he thought Hornswoggle was Wee-Man. So he got called Wee-Man two times in less than twenty-four hours. Boy, was he mad.

Do You Work Out?

Beth Phoenix

To your average person, if they go on the road, they're away from home. But the amount we travel, I would say that you have to adapt to the road so that it feels like home. So you start to pick up little habits and nuances so that you feel like you're living a normal life on the road. You need to have a regimen so that you can feel normal anywhere you are on the road anywhere around the world. So for myself, in particular, a big part of my character and a big part of what I do is staying in shape. A lot of times, for me, the biggest challenge is actually just trying to find a gym or someplace to work out. I need more than a Curves, so most of the time I need to turn to the male Superstars to find the best places to work out. The type of training that I do is strength training and power lifting, so I need a serious gym. For the most part, that's my focus when I get on the road. That's how I find my sense of normalcy, through training. Constantly working out on the road is really the only way we can keep our bodies healthy—and eating, that's a whole other issue when we're on the road. You have to prepare yourself with healthy things to eat, you have to carry around healthy foods with you so you're not stuck in Mobile, Alabama, somewhere and your only options are eating Ho Hos and Ding Dongs at the Kwik-E-Mart down the street.

What I've noticed is that everyone carries things with them to remind them of home. I know some of my friends on the road, some of the guys will set up their area in the locker room really meticulously, and they do this on a regular basis. They put their boots in a certain place every time, they have their bag open a certain way, and it's their way to make their own special space in the locker room. It feels like your space because it's your stuff and it's set up the same way. It's just another way to try and find that normalcy. Maybe when you're home, the first thing you do is plop down on your couch. Well, when you get to your hotel, maybe you always plop down on your bed and turn on the TV or you set up your area in the locker room the same particular way just so you have that home away from home.

I know for me, though, on the road I'm all about business. I'm all about eating well, sleeping well, and training. That's how I feel like I've kept myself healthy and strong. I don't take shopping trips or do any of that girlie stuff on the road.

It's funny, though, because since my character is very aggressive on the show and pretty mean, when I meet people I think they're surprised I'm not trying to eat their face off. Obviously, unless I'm competing in the ring, I have no reason to stomp around and punch people. But for myself, personally, the single most annoying icebreaker line that I get all the time is, "Hey, do you work out?" I get this from men and women, mostly men, of course, and I get it constantly at the gym. I'll be lifting heavy weights, and in the middle of my workout, someone will come over with the "Hey, do you work out?" line. They'll be like, "Are you a bodybuilder or something?" I always want to say something like, "No, I'm a baker." It's just one of those things where you know people mean well, but it's the silliest thing on earth to say. It's actually become somewhat of a big joke to me now, just because I get it so much. So I take it with a grain of salt and politely explain to people what I do for a living. It's so funny, though, because I can see people staring at me, and I can see them kind of start creeping over, and I already know what they're going to say. And nine times out of ten, there it is, "Do you work out?"

On the flip side, it really means a lot to me when little kids come up to me and want to talk to me because that's what I got in this business to do, to be an inspiration to the little guys. That's what wrestling was for me growing up. It wasn't just this great form of entertainment. I was really inspired to become a better person and to listen to the messages the Superstars said. It was also a time of great bonding for myself and my family when I was growing up, so for now, to be a part of that, and to be able to work for WWE and to have the honor and pleasure to see my picture on the side of the trucks when I drive up to the building . . . It never ceases to blow my mind to see my face on the back of the truck and working for WWE, when I used to have Stone Cold and Bret Hart and the British Bulldog and Lex Luger pictures plastered all over my walls as a kid. Now, here I am, I get to be one of those faces. It's pretty incredible.

Get the Horns

R-Truth

I travel with a bunch of different people, sometimes Jimmy Wang Yang or Jeff Hardy, sometimes Shane Helms or Vladimir Kozlov. It alternates. But I remember one day a few of us were driving and I saw a cow on the side of the road. I made a comment to Brian Kendrick that if he pulled over, I would jump out and go ride that cow. He didn't even need to think about it. Next thing I know, he pulls a U-turn in the middle of the street, and we're headed back to the cow. So I had to do it now. Only thing is, when I got out of the car and started walking toward it, it turned around, and it wasn't a cow . . . it was a bull! It started huffing at us and looking mean, so we all jumped back in the car and got out of there. That was one of the weirdest things I've ever seen. I never thought I'd get that close to a bull.

When we left, Vladimir turned to me and said, "You picked the wrong target."

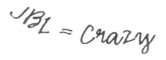

JBL = Crazy

D'Lo Brown

I remember this one time I was in a car with Taka and Mark Henry. We were up in Newfoundland. It was around midnight, and we were making a two-hour drive between cities. All I remember about the road was that it was about as desolate a highway as you could find, and it was pitch black. I'm doing like 80 mph because I want to get to the hotel, then all of a sudden I get bumped. I look up in my mirror, and it's Bradshaw, and he's cackling in the driver's seat, and sitting next to him is Ron Simmons. Taka was asleep in the back, and he bursts up, looks behind him to see Bradshaw, and yells, "Oh no, Bradshaw, that guy is crazy!" So now we're at this high-speed run at about 110 mph, and Bradshaw is still bumping us from behind. Taka turned white as a sheet, Mark Henry is just sitting there laughing, and I'm panicking thinking we're going to roll the car or smash into something. The funniest part of the whole race was Taka's reaction. "Bradshaw, he's crazy!"

That's all Taka kept saying, even when we finally made it back to the hotel. And he's right, Bradshaw is crazy.

The Little Man Is a Little (Lot) Weird

Tommy Dreamer

I was sharing a room with a guy, and he was single, and he ended up bringing a girl back to the room with him. We were also sharing a room with Hornswoggle at the time, but I got to the room first and just threw a bunch of pillows on the floor next to my bed and fell asleep before anyone else had gotten to the room. Anyway, this guy comes in the room with the girl, and they start "hanging out," when all of a sudden Hornswoggle popped up from underneath the bed. I never knew he was there, the other guy didn't know he was there, and obviously the girl didn't know he was there, so we all started screaming. And the way Hornswoggle popped up, it looked like he was coming from under the bed, just like he does when he's hiding under the ring for one of our shows. He really scared the crap out of all of us.

But that's not all. For some reason, maybe because

he's weird, Hornswoggle will get up in the middle of the night, take a pillow, and go sleep on the cold floor in the middle of the bathroom. He says he likes it really, really cold. So when I would get up to go to the bathroom in the middle of the night, I would see a dead little manatee on the floor, and it would be Hornswoggle, 'cause that's what he looks like. There was even this one time when I went to go to the bathroom and Hornswoggle was asleep on the toilet bowl, 'cause he's just a weird little man.

What a Drag

Maria

One time I got to the building early, so I figured I'd go sign some autographs. I put my bags down, because no one was around except for the guys driving the big WWE trucks. Unfortunately, the driver wanted to go and he didn't see my luggage, so he backs over my luggage, and the fans are screaming, "He's running over your luggage!" I turn around, and my bags are getting dragged down the street by the truck. Thank God my dog wasn't with me or that would've been a whole other problem. I probably would've killed the guy. Luckily, I left my dog home that trip so he avoided getting run over by our huge semi.

Wrestling's Number-One Sports Fan

MVP

One of the toughest parts about being on the road so much is trying to keep up with the scores of my favorite sports teams. I'm a lifelong Raiders fan. It breaks my heart the way they've been playing, but I bleed silver and black. And oddly enough, growing up in Miami when Miami didn't have a baseball team or a basketball team or a hockey team, I ended up becoming a fan of all the New York teams because when we got cable TV, we ended up getting all of New York's programming. My mom's friend's husband used to sit me on the couch back when I was in second grade, and we'd watch the Yankees, the Rangers, and the Knicks. And my teams have been my teams since I was little. I'm not a bandwagon fan. I stay true to my teams, and you can tell that just by the fact that I'm a Raiders fan and a Knicks fan at the same time. It's torture. Another team I'm really into is Manchester United of the English Premier League. I get a lot of flak for that because Manchester United is like the Yankees of the English Premier League. People in Manchester don't even root for Manchester United. I even came out on *Raw* one night with a Manchester United jersey on. I got into a little trouble for that, but they're my team.

So while I'm on the road, I have constant score updates on my BlackBerry, then when I get to the hotel I'll catch the highlights on ESPN. I'm constantly pulling up scores and highlights online. And in terms of college sports, I'm a die-hard Miami Hurricanes fan . . . I see a national title in our future.

But man, back to the Raiders, Rey Mysterio and I always have our friendly wagers, because he's a big Chargers fan and the Raiders play the Chargers twice a year. But because the Raiders have been so bad for so long now, I'm so far in the hole to him, I don't think I can ever get out. We usually bet a hundred bucks a game. Lucky we only play twice a year. We're so bad I can't even talk trash. I just hand him my money. I wouldn't even mind losing if the Raiders played tough like the old days. Maybe they'd lose, but people at least feared them. They lost that mystique a long time ago. I don't think the Raiders will rise again until Al Davis dies. It's sad to say, but it's the truth.

Will the Real Rey please Stand Up?

Rey Mysterio

I always put my mask on about half a block before I pull up to the building. That way, when I drive up to the arena, I have my mask on. Just recently, though, we were wrestling at a casino and I was the last guy to leave the building. I was by myself that day, and I walked out without my mask on, put my bags in the car, and I heard some fans out there who were yelling, "Rey! Rey! Please sign!" So I walked over and signed autographs for everybody, and eventually I ran into this little boy whose parents were there and they asked me if I could take a picture with their son. I was like, "Yeah, no problem." But this kid, he was looking at me strange, and he just kept saying, "No, that's not Rey. That's not Rey." So I showed him my tattoos, and usually kids will figure out who I am by my tattoos, but this boy, he still didn't believe me. He was pleading, "This isn't Rey. I want Rey with the mask." So I walked back to my car, put my mask on, and came back out to take a picture with him. I took the picture, signed some more autographs, and I could see him staring at me. He still couldn't decide whether he believed it was me or not. His parents were trying to convince him the whole time and I stayed to talk to him for a bit and I think finally he came around, but it was funny how this kid just kept saying, "No, that's not him. I'm not taking a picture with this guy. I want a picture with Rey."

Punch Heard 'Round the Amusement Park

Cody Rhodes

I've known Santino Marella since we came up together in OVW in Louisville, Kentucky. One day, back when we were in Louisville, we decided to talk our wrestling trainers into letting us go to Six Flags. It should have been no big deal. We had been training hard. I had been on the road to a couple of different live events and showed my skills or what have you . . . I showed what I had to the WWE's top brass. We were all vying for that spot, and we wanted to go out and have some fun.

So we approached our trainers with the premise that we were all going to be on our best behavior. This rowdy bunch of pro wrestlers just wasn't going to act like that at the park. We were all going to maintain, have a good time, ride some rides, and eat some junk food. Again, we were all working hard and we needed a day off.

So when we go and get our tickets, we have this meeting about being on our best behavior. And I have to emphasize, we had more than one meeting about this. When we were back at the OVW building, we had a meeting about being on our best behavior. When we got to the park, we are told to be on our best behavior. They couldn't have emphasized the importance of this any more.

But then we get to the park.

Not eleven seconds into being in the park, I turn around and I see the Tasmanian Devil character from the WB, and it's clawing in the air, waving its hands around. Then I see the handler, another park employee, just screaming at Santino Marella.

Turns out Santino got a little excited when he walked in, and he decided to give the Tasmanian Devil a one-two punch right in the mask. Here's the best part: As our trainers are walking in our direction, I know we're all in trouble, and Santino is trying to talk his way out of it, but then the Tasmanian Devil lifts off its head and it's a little girl inside. Not like ten years old, she was probably like fourteen, fifteen . . . whatever the minimum age for a park employee to work there. And she just had tears streaming down her face.

I've never seen a bigger look of disappointment in anyone's face as the look I saw from Santino. It was really the funniest thing I can recall. He was quarantined to the wave pool the rest of the day. He sat there the entire day with the boo-hoo face of all boo-hoo faces.

Eight

Back in the Day

"There were times I wrestled in front of twelve or fifteen people, but I performed like I was in front of fifty thousand people."

—REY MYSTERIO

Think spiders crawling in your bed, rental cars spinning into ditches, and hotel keys hitting you in the eye are bad? That's nothing compared to what it took these Superstars to actually make it to the top. From performing in barns and high-school gymnasiums to getting excited when there were two hundred people in the crowd to lying about your age just so you could sneak into a bar to perfect your craft in front of a smattering of drunks, the following are a few stories from life on the road before the Superstars became household names. ✿ This is what paying your dues is all about.

Bringing Home the Bacon

Christian

I know when I was coming up, Owen Hart helped me out and took me under his wing. I lived in Canada at the time and he lived in Calgary, so a lot of times he would have to connect in Toronto, so we would end up on the same flights from Toronto and we'd sit next to each other and talk a lot. He would teach me a lot about the road and little tricks on how to make life easier when we travel. It meant a lot to me when I first got with the company for a guy like Owen to sit down and help me out like he did.

It's crazy though, because when I was first starting out on the Independents, you never knew what to expect. You might have a two-hour drive and end up wrestling in front of fifty people. If you're lucky, you're wrestling in front of six hundred people. At the same time, you're not making any money, so you're sharing a hotel room with five or six other guys. You're squished into somebody's car and you're just trying to save enough money to eat. That's what changes when you get to WWE. Now you're flying most places and you can afford a nice rental car, a nice hotel, and a nice meal.

I wrestled once inside a barn in Tennessee in front of like fifteen people. The guy who ran the show, it was inside his dad's barn, and I remember during the middle of the show, his dad came home with groceries and was walking through the crowd with groceries under his arms, shoving through people to get to his house that was attached to the barn. He was trying to put his groceries away while the match was going on. It was pretty funny.

Keep Your Mask On

Rey Mysterio

My first road trips were from San Diego to L.A. at the age of fourteen. Back then, I had to wear my mask because we would wrestle in bars and they would sneak me in through the back because I was underage. They would tell me, "Rey, put your mask on and don't take it off. Keep your mask on at all times, and if someone asks, tell them you're just a short wrestler or a midget." Whatever I did, I couldn't take my mask off. Back then it was a trip, because here I was sneaking into bars and I was wrestling guys twice my age.

And the people who were at these bars, they showed

very little interest in the matches anyway. In my case, I had to win these people over with my wrestling style. It's not like we were wrestling in these bars with any big names. So back then, I was doing so much high-flying because not a whole lot of people who were there knew much about wrestling, but they would go crazy over any little dive or special headscissor or Frankensteiner. They would go crazy for those moves, and it was cool for me to break in that way. All my first road trips were either to wrestle at bars or to wrestle outside churches in Mexico, and you have to think, back then all I wanted was the opportunity to step in the ring. I didn't care if it was five people or five hundred people. There were times I wrestled in front of twelve or fifteen people, but I performed like I was in front of fifty thousand people. Every time I step into the ring, it's about putting on the best show possible for the fans. It's been quite a road.

Two Different Worlds

MVP

It's kind of disappointing when you're wrestling in front of twenty or thirty people, but still, you lace 'em up because what you have to realize is, even in front of that many people, you're still learning your craft. So then, when you wrestled in front of two hundred people, you were like, "Wow, we have a good house tonight." Oftentimes I actually stop and reflect, thinking about when I first started and wrestled in a hall in front of thirty people. Then I think about being in Ford Field at *Wrestle-Mania* in front of eighty thousand people, with millions more at home tuning in. Talk about one extreme to the other. But whether there's twenty people or twenty thousand people, it all comes down to the fact that, hey, these people all bought a ticket and they're here to be entertained. And it's my job to entertain them. Now, the adrenaline rush will certainly get you more pumped up in front of a larger crowd, but honestly, there's no difference in my performance between two thousand and twenty thousand . . . I do what I do. Sometimes it hurts less in front of twenty thousand people just because you're so amped up, but the fans make it all worthwhile: the bumps, the bruises, the travel. At the end of my match, win, lose, or draw, when the crowd chants "M-V-P," there isn't anything better than that.

The WWE universe is very demanding. They know garbage from the goods, they know what they're watching. The fans, they decide: We like him, they cheer me, and to me, that's one of the coolest things that could happen. Fans walk up to me all the time in the hotel and they tell me, "You're a future World Champion." I just tell them, "I hope so."

nine

Legacy

"Sure, it's tough sometimes, but we love what we do."

—RANDY ORTON

"The wrestling industry is one big cycle," Randy Orton explains, dissecting what it means to live life on the road and make the sacrifices necessary to hit it big in WWE. **"When you start out, when you're a new guy, if you have potential and one of the older guys in the locker room sees that, a lot of times they'll guide you and take you under their wing,"** he says, helping sum up one of the most overlooked but vitally important aspects of the time shared together on the road. ❂ **You see, riding in rental cars around the world isn't just about finding your way to the arena and to the top of the business (or about bad hotels, or even worse food), it's about**

helping out your fellow Superstars along the way. It's about those four-hour drives breaking down matches and story lines as you talk about your relationships and family back at home with your adopted family on the road.

It's about doing whatever is in your power to live your dream, while everyone in your car is living theirs right alongside of you.

Nobody does a better job talking about this lifestyle and what it means than third-generation Superstar Randy Orton.

So I leave you with his words. Maybe the most important in the book if you're looking for that one thing that makes the wrestling industry continue to tick (and I'm not talking about anything Randy bought in Mexico).

Leaving a Legacy

Randy Orton

When I was coming up along with John Cena and Brock Lesnar, we all had our mentors. I was lucky because Triple H singled me out. I'll never forget, one day he saw me practicing in the ring. I was locked in a figure-four, and the cameras weren't on, but it was the way I was selling — the move that he really liked. From what he saw, I was sell-

Woodbury
Roxbury Falls
Brookfield
Southbury
South Britain
Haviland
Putnam Lake
New Fairfield
Brookfield Center
Sandy Hook
Hawleyville
Weston
Pound Ridge
Wilton
S. Wilton
Green-field Hill
New Canaan
Long Ridge
Bridge-port
North Stamford
Winnipauk
Westport
Fairfield
Norwalk
Southport
Saugatuck
Greens Farms
East Norwalk
Darien
South Norwalk
Rowayton
Noroton
Stamford
Old Greenwich
Riverside

ing the figure-four the way it should be done. So after I got out of the ring, he pulled me aside and told me he'd been watching me and that he wanted to start this group and he'd get back to me on it. Eventually that group became Evolution. So I got to ride with Evolution and ride with Ric Flair and ride with Triple H, and I learned so much from these guys. At first Batista wasn't in, and it was just me, Ric, and Hunter, and we had so much fun in New York City, riding around in limos and flying around in helicopters in order to shoot the video package for our entrance. And I really got the chance to bond with these guys, and they told me about things inside the ring, outside the ring, how to act, how to be a locker room leader. Eventually, one day I knew that it would be my turn to take somebody under my wing. That's the way it goes. Every so often a new wave of guys comes in, and that time is now. I used to be the young guy, but now I see these younger guys coming in who are four to eight years younger than I am already.

When I look at guys like Cody and Ted and Kofi Kingston—who is my opponent—I'm in a position to help make these guys. Then eventually, they'll be in that position as well. It's a learning process. Being successful in this business takes time. Unless you're a golden boy or a Brock Lesnar or someone who can just be thrown right into the mix right away, you have to work at it. It's a building process. And it's not something that just takes a couple of years. It took me a good five to six years before people started believing in me, and there are so many aspects to that: coming up with a finishing move, having a move set that people recognize, having a character that you believe in and are confident in, so that when you walk through that curtain and walk onto that stage, those fans watching you know by the look in your eyes that you mean business. They know that they can believe in this character. That's really what you need to do . . . find a character you can have confidence in. When a new guy walks to the ring, you can sense that nervous energy. He doesn't know what to do, so he's looking around, and you can tell he's not confident in himself. And when a wrestler isn't confident in himself, it's hard for him to get over because the fans can sense that. Right away they'll crap on that because it's no good. They're not paying for that. They're paying to have reality suspended. They want to believe in something. They want us to put on a show that they can get wrapped up into and lost in. They want to believe.

That's where a lot of these critics come in and call wrestling fake. To me, that's the most disrespectful thing anyone can say. I've seen Hunter tear both quads, his groin, and get his throat crushed. I've had two shoulder surgeries, a broken foot, a nasty dislocation, broken digits, jaw problems, a broken collarbone, concussions . . . and that's average. Guys have had neck surgeries and broken arms, lots of knee problems and back issues. So to call this fake, that's like a slap in the face. We love what we do. It's not like your normal nine-to-five in some office where you dream of working somewhere else. We get to travel and see the world. And sure, it's tough sometimes, but we love what we do. And the guys who love what they do and who have the hearts for it, they're the ones who are able to channel those passions. A lot of times lately, there are guys coming up who are second and third generation. These are guys who were born into the business, and they have that respect. There are all kinds of ex–football players and ex-Olympians in training camp now, but when they come up, we call them the Tin Men because they don't have hearts. That's a nasty little moniker that they've been given, but it's true. You have to know this world. And you have to want to protect it and know what's best for it. Guys with big heads and egos come in, and they don't know any better, but their career is over just like that, and they never understand. But you have to do what's right to make each other look good. You have to do what's best for the business.

Ted and Cody, Kofi Kingston, Harry Smith, Tyson Kidd, and Nattie Neidhart . . . people like that who come up, they have the heart. Mike Rotunda's two boys who are training, Taylor and Windham, they have the heart. They are training in FCW right now, but they are about to become part of that cycle where the young and hungry come up with all that potential and all that talent, and it's up to guys like me, guys like Hunter and John Cena and guys who have been a part of this cycle, to step in and help these young guys out. And eventually there's another wave and another wave. That's just how sports entertainment thrives. And a lot of those lessons that need to be taught, they're not learned inside the ring. They're learned on the road.

Acknowledgments

I'd like to thank all of the WWE Superstars and Divas who met

with me in various hotels and arenas throughout the country

to share their thoughts and stories from life on the road. I'd

also like to thank all of those stars who called on their days

off to fill me in on the tour's most recent ribs, rental car wrecks,

and hotel horrors. Special thanks go out to Dean Miller for

all of the introductions, Mike Archer for hooking up his boy

"Ballgame," and Jaime Jensen for helping set up my first road

trip (and breaking the gas cap off the rental). As someone

who grew up a follower of everything Ricky Steamboat,

it's amazing to see the experience from the other side

of the curtain, and no fan should ever take for granted the sacrifices (both physical and mental) each of these men and women make in order to entertain the WWE universe.

To Kofi Kingston: One day I'm going to show you how a true *Madden* abbot plays the game. And Randy, you owe me a ride on that bus.

To the B-Man and Sunshine, thanks for going to bed early so Dad could finish his book. Your WWE Title and Divas Championship will be ready in about eighteen years. Extra special thanks to my wife, Nicole, who makes the return of my every road trip that much more special.

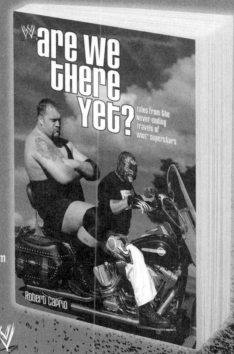